CREOLES AND COOLIES;

OR,

FIVE YEARS IN MAURITIUS.

BY THE

REV. PATRICK BEATON, M.A.

Second Edition.

KENNIKAT PRESS
Port Washington, N. Y./London

CREOLES AND COOLIES

First published in 1859
Reissued in 1971 by Kennikat Press
Library of Congress Catalog Card No: 77-118457
ISBN 0-8046-1207-2

Manufactured by Taylor Publishing Company   Dallas, Texas

KENNIKAT NEGRO CULTURE AND HISTORY SERIES

PREFACE.

In this work, which embodies the experience derived from a residence of more than five years in the colony, the author has endeavoured to present a lively but faithful picture of the impressions produced upon a stranger by the mixed and motley population of Mauritius; to describe the working of slavery, and the present condition of the ex-slave population and their descendants; to trace the connexion between the present prosperity of the colony, and the introduction of Coolie immigrants from India; and to point out the advantages which it possesses as a field for missionary labour among these men. If the

publication of this work result in engaging
the sympathies of the religious world at home
in behalf of these Coolies, by attracting attention to their spiritual destitution, and to the
powerful influence which their conversion to
Christianity may exercise upon the future
evangelisation of India, and thus lead, in any
measure, to the extension of the means already
in operation for bringing the gospel within
their reach, the author's object will be fully
accomplished.

LONDON, *August* 1858.

CONTENTS.

CHAPTER IV.

CHAPTER V.

CHAPTER VI.

CHAPTER VII.

CHAPTER VIII.

CREOLES AND COOLIES.

CHAPTER I.

THE appearance of Mauritius, as you approach it by sea,
is very striking and romantic. It is intersected in different directions by chains of mountains, most of which
are covered with verdure to the summit, and end in the
most fantastic peaks, as if Nature had been in a merry
mood at the moment of their creation. Sometimes
the peaks of the Pieter Both and Pouce are seen from
an immense distance at sea, more especially when the
lower parts of the island are covered with vapour. The
mountain-tops then assume the form of eyries, perched

aloft amongst the clouds; but when the wind rises and the vapour passes away, land is no longer visible, and the mariner is tempted to believe himself the victim of some magical delusion. The Pouce derives its name from its resemblance to the thumb, and the Pieter Both from a silly Dutchman, who, trying to scale its heights, met with his death in the attempt.* Others, however, have tried the ascent with better success than the heavy Dutchman, and the Union Jack has twice floated on its rocky peak, to the disgust of the *habitans*, who believed it inaccessible. An interesting account of the ascent of the mountain was published in the *Penny Magazine* by Colonel Lloyd, who was for some years Surveyor-General in Mauritius, and died of cholera in the Crimea. The three principal ranges of mountains were formerly covered with wood, the most of which has now been cut down, and the inhabitants complain, with reason, that this destruction has had a pernicious effect upon the climate and fruitfulness of the colony. Latterly the Government have appointed an Inspector of Woods and Forests, with a number of *gardes champêtres* under his command; but the evil cannot now be remedied; and, even with this precaution, the quantity of wood on the island is diminishing every year. There is a corresponding diminution in the fall of rain; and unless something be done through planting, and more stringent measures for the preservation of the trees, the cultivation of sugar, the staple article of produce, may at some future period be aban-

* Others derive the name from a Dutch Admiral.

doned, and Mauritius become a barren rock, inhabited only by a few fishermen. The town of Port Louis is situated in a species of hollow, surrounded on three sides by mountains, or nearly so. Its situation is very low, and the excellent harbour could alone have led to the selection of its site. Its superiority over that of Grand Port is evident, and the only ground for surprise is, that the Dutch, a maritime people, should ever have selected Grand Port as their capital, in preference to Port Louis. A ship on arriving is obliged to lie at anchor at the Bell Buoy until the visiting doctor has come on board to examine the bill of health, and given the ship what is technically called *pratique*. Although we arrived at five P.M., and this official ought, in virtue of his office, to visit all ships that arrive before six, we had no visit from him before eight o'clock the following morning.

The harbour of Port Louis affords safe and ample anchorage to ships of the largest burden. It is, therefore, very convenient for those ships bound for or from India that fall short of provisions, or have been caught in one of those hurricanes with which this quarter of the globe is periodically visited. Two patent-slip docks have been built, in which the largest vessels can receive repairs. Ships requiring such repairs are obliged to put in at Mauritius, or to return to Bombay, there being no other intermediate port suitable to their wants. Hence it is no unusual thing, after a hurricane at sea, for the harbour of Port Louis to be crowded with English, French, and American ships, undergoing

or waiting for repairs, and the profits made by the
proprietors of these docks are enormous.   The merchants to whom these ships are consigned receive a
very handsome commission ; and, perhaps, some of
them regard a good thorough-paced hurricane with
much the same feelings as a farmer, with a large stock
of grain in his barns, looked upon a heavy fall of snow
in harvest—" Oh, my friends, let us be thankful for this
precious weather."   The harbour has something of
the shape of a horse-shoe, with the cleft or open part
towards the sea.   It is one of the best and safest
harbours in the East, but sadly neglected.   Every
species of filth is allowed to accumulate in it, rendering
its neighbourhood very unwholesome, and offensive to
more senses than one.   Fever and cholera find appropriate abodes in the hovels situated near the Trou
Fanfaron and its other precincts.   It is asserted also,
and the fact appears to be undeniable, that it has been
gradually diminishing in depth, owing to neglect in
clearing away the *débris* that accumulates in its bed,
more especially during the period of the heavy rains.
Besides the River Lataniers, which enters the harbour
in several small streamlets, there are other rivulets of
smaller importance, which empty themselves into the
basin.   During the rainy season, the sides of the
mountains and the banks of these streams are washed
by the torrents that descend—the loose earth, sand,
and even stones of a large size, are swept into their
beds, and borne along by the force of the current ;
and thus a considerable quantity of solid matter is

conveyed every season to the harbour, for the removal of which no adequate measures have been adopted. The accumulation of this *débris* has been so great within a few years, that where there were twenty-four feet of water there are now only sixteen; and unless some steps be adopted to check this growing evil, it may be that, in the course of time, none but ships of the smallest size will be able to find an entrance.

A boat came alongside soon after our arrival, and offered to land passengers. Of course, this was very tantalising, as none could leave the ship before the doctor's visit. It contained the first specimens of the Creole race that I had seen; and as they were fair representatives of a class, I may describe them. Their complexion was a rich olive-brown, their eyes dark and intelligent, their features well-formed and regular, their faces long rather than oval, and their hair dark and curly—a sure proof of the presence of African blood. Their figures were long and lithe, giving one the impression of activity rather than of strength, and so erect as to prove that they had little experience of severe physical labour. They wore jackets of a blue Indian cloth, shirts of dazzling whiteness, and neat straw-hats, which they politely and gracefully raised from their heads when addressed. They addressed me in something like the following terms:—" Si Monsieur content débarquer, nous voulè prenne li dans le bateau." * I could only shake my head in token of refusal.

* "If Monsieur wishes to go ashore, we'll take him in the boat."

The first view of Port Louis gives you the idea of a large garden, with houses scattered through it at long intervals, with a few public buildings peeping through the foliage. This effect results from the trees and gardens with which most of the better class of houses are surrounded. Facing the harbour are the Custom-house and Civil Hospital, large white buildings, with no pretensions to architectural beauty. Near the Civil Hospital is the lofty square tower (one of the first objects seen on entering the harbour) of St Andrew's Church. In the centre of the town stands Government House, which the uninitiated would naturally take to be a large sugar-store, from its ugliness and utter want of architectural ornament. Farther on, in the direction of the Champ de Mars, is the Roman Catholic Cathedral, a solid, compact building, of no particular style of architecture ; and near it, but more to the right, the English Cathedral, originally a powder magazine, but now converted to more peaceful purposes. On the right is a suburb, composed of miserable-looking huts, extending along the base of the signal mountain, inhabited by negroes, and known as Black Town. To the left another suburb, stretching out for nearly half-a-mile in the direction of Pamplemousses, the favourite abode of the Indian population, known as Malabar Town. On the right the town is overlooked by the signal mountain, on the left by the citadel; while behind is the green expanse of the Champ de Mars, encompassed with neat villas, and the valley of the Pouce, with its old military road leading to the Chateau d'Eau. There are two forts, for the protection of the entrance of the harbour, and two martello towers erected at the mouth of Grand River. The first impression of Port Louis is not very favourable. It seems an accumulation of houses and huts heaped together without order or plan, and is destitute of any of those public buildings which, by their splendour and beauty, give an air of interest to the smaller provincial towns in Europe. It reminds one of the descriptions of Rome in the days of Romulus, and its population is even more mixed and motley than that which flocked to the newly-erected capital of Latium.

All at once the sun sunk beneath the western horizon, lighting up in his departure the summit of the Pouce, which seemed pointing aloft in admiration of his beauty, and tinting with his golden rays the statue of Victoria with her crown and coronation robes, or rather the striking resemblance to her Majesty assumed by the peak of the Pieter Both, when seen from the sea. The setting of the tropical sun suggests the lines of the poet —lines which prove that genius can realise, through the power of imagination alone, scenes described by others, with the same vivid truthfulness as if they were the objects of actual perception. Millions daily see the setting of the tropical sun, but none have described it so well as Scott, who saw it only with the mind's eye:—

> " Mine be the eve of tropic sun—
> No pale gradations quench his ray,
> No twilight dews his wrath allay,
> With disk, like battle-target red,
> He rushes to his burning bed,
> Dyes the wide wave with bloody light,
> Then sinks at once—and all is night."

One's feelings, on arriving in a new country, are generally of a very mixed character. You feel as if you were about to cast off all old associations and to enter upon a new mode of existence. Old memories of kind faces, loving hearts, and scenes long past and apparently forgotten, come rushing tumultuously upon the mind, as if they felt that their hold was loosening, and that they must speedily give place to others. With curiosity to examine the land of your sojourning for a time, there is a yearning of the heart for a land still dearer, and even the old ship, which you may have daily characterised as a tub, for her slowness, is left with something of regret. You feel like the patriarch of old, who went out not knowing whither he went; and you are ignorant of what fate may be in store for you. You have a memento of the uncertainty of life and all its plans in the cemetery close at hand, where many brave young British hearts, once beating high with courage and hope as much as yours, are now mouldering to dust on a foreign strand, with none to lament them. You hear the wailing sound of the wind passing through the *filaos*,* those graceful and appropriate ornaments of the city of the dead. In the days of ancient mythology an Ovid might have represented them as the mothers of the dead weeping over them, and changed by some pitying god into their present shape.

But now the evening gun has fired, and its reverberations, after being caught up and repeated by the mountains behind, like the rolling of thunder, have died away

* The casuarina of Madagascar.

in the distance. The merry song of the sailors heaving the anchor has ceased. The silence of night is only interrupted by the dirge-like song of some watchful Coolie, by the beating of a distant tom-tom, and a howling of dogs, so general and so long continued, as to tempt the belief that I had arrived at some island inhabited only by those sagacious animals, such as some of our early mariners have described.

It was in vain that I tried to sleep. Between heat, mosquitoes, the howling of dogs, and the excitement resulting from the circumstances in which I found myself, my nervous system became so excited as effectually to banish sleep from my eyelids. I had no help for it, but to walk the deck till the report of the gun from the citadel announced the approach of morn. The night was soft and beautiful. The clear bright moon, with softened rays, left a track of silver upon the ocean, while she dimly disclosed the mountains in all their romantic beauty. The firmament shone forth with its stars, surpassing in brilliancy those seen in northern climes, and explaining how the East gave birth to astronomy, astrology, and sabaism. One can understand in gazing upon such a scene how the Orientals, with their dim traditional ideas of Deity, in the patriarchal age, when beholding the moon walking in brightness, felt their hearts enticed, and their mouths disposed to kiss their hands in adoration of the queen of heaven.

But now it is eight o'clock, and the doctor and landing-officer have come on board. Our bill of health is examined, and found satisfactory. Gracious permission is given to us to land, of which we speedily avail ourselves. A boat, rowed by two coloured men, with crispy hair and sepia complexions, speedily conveys me ashore. Their charge for rowing me about a quarter of a mile is so exorbitant as to give some air of truth to what I had previously been told, that no man, black or white, in Mauritius, will open his mouth to answer even in a monosyllable for less than a dollar. On landing, the first thing that strikes a stranger is the primitive manner in which the inhabitants are dressed. He sees the wharf thronged with men occupied in different ways, whose movements are quite unimpeded by those tightly fitting garments which are worn by Europeans. He is not disposed to form a high opinion of the refinement or civilisation of the inhabitants of Mauritius, from the specimens that are first brought under his notice. He must not confound these half-naked, savage-looking men, with the Creoles of Mauritius, or do them the injustice to suppose that the art of dress has reached no higher degree of perfection. He must reserve his opinion, and mingle for some time in Mauritius society, and he shall yet see coats such as Stultz might have cut, and toilettes so perfect, that they might do honour to the Chaussée d'Antin or the procession of Longchamps. Those scantily-clad, turbaned wretches, whom in our ignorance we have mistaken for the refined and highly civilised Mauritians, are Coolies from the banks of the Ganges, brought hither to be hewers of wood and drawers of water; to do the work of Helots for three years, and to be so, all but in name. Those swarthy Orientals, so thinly clad, are the muscles and sinews of the Mauritius body politic. They are the secret source of all the wealth, luxury, and splendour with which the island abounds. There is not a carriage that rolls along the well-macadamised Chaussée, or a robe of silk worn by the fair Mauritian, to the purchase of which the Indian has not, by his labour, indirectly contributed. It is from the labour of his swarthy body in the cane-fields that gold is extracted more plenteously than from the diggings of Ballarat. Respect that swarthy stranger, for without him Mauritius would soon be stripped of its wealth, and left with scarcely sufficient exports to procure food for its rice-eating, cigar-smoking inhabitants. We pass the poor Coolies (to return to them again) with the simple reflection, that if half of this be true, their masters might procure them a more decent clothing, and thus avoid shocking the delicacy of every lady that lands on their shores.

The Indian women wear a dress which seems to be composed of one piece of cotton cloth, wrapped round the middle, forming a short petticoat reaching to the knee, with the ends flung loosely over the shoulders, so as to cover the breast. They appear a degraded race of beings, with the worst passions painted in their coarse, revolting, unwomanly features. The only redeeming feature in their character is their seeming fondness for their children. These are not carried on the back, or in the arms, as in Europe, but perched astride on the left haunch, which is protruded for the purpose of supporting them, and there they sit grinning and shewing their white teeth, while the mothers waddle along with their bodies in shape something like the letter C.

To the European, ignorant of the types and costumes of the different Oriental races, nothing can be more striking than the appearance of the Mauritians. The first impression of surprise and wonder speedily wears off, and the mind becomes accustomed to the diversity of language, colour, and race. But on first landing, if at all of an imaginative character, he may conceive himself in the capital of the Caliphs, and surrounded with all the witchery of Eastern romance. So overpowering is the feeling of novelty, that if a mute were to sign to him to follow, he would follow as a matter of course; and if after being conducted through gardens bubbling with fountains, and loaded with golden fruit, he found himself in a bath-room, floored with marble, he would resign himself without resistance to the hands of the attendants, ready to untwist every joint of his body in the process of shampooing. He sees faces rendered familiar to his imagination in childhood by the charming pages of the Arabian Nights, or such as the old masters have given to the heroes and the patriarchs of a still more wonderful volume. He sees Arabs from the shores of the Red Sea, whose dress, features, and language have undergone little change from the friction of forty cen-

turies—who retain, in the midst of civilised life, something of the freedom of the desert—and who cherish the
reminiscences of their former nomad life by surrounding themselves with the horses of their native land.
He sees haughty Mohammedans, descendants of a race
who conquered India before the English flag was ever
unfurled on its shores—men tall of stature, muscular
in build, with regular features, lofty brows, bull-like
necks, and flowing beards.   He sees Indians from the
burning plains of Hindostan, weak and effeminate in
frame, soft and gentle in expression, fawning and servile in address, with their dark, curling locks, longer
and glossier than those that adorned the heads of the
Roman youth during the reign of the later emperors.
He sees Chinamen from the Celestial Empire, attracted
to the abode of the barbarian by the *sacra fames
auri*—a grotesque-looking race, with long faces, wide
mouths, flattened noses, high cheek-bones, and curious
eyes, shaped like button-holes, wearing trousers of the
same portentous size as Peter the Headstrong, with each
leg large enough to contain the whole body, and abjur-
ing long locks, save a single one on the crown of the
head, plaited and pendulous, or twisted round the head,
according to the taste of the wearer.   He sees dark
descendants of Ham, of all types and countries inhabited by that servile race : ex-apprentices, fast sinking
into the grave, often halt and lame and maimed, bearing in their decrepid, toil-worn bodies a stronger argument against slavery than ever issued from the eloquent
lips of Wilberforce or Brougham ; free negroes, the

offspring of slaves, plump, shiny, and good-humoured, but devoid of ambition, foresight, honesty and truth; Malagashes, of two different nations, the one agreeing in physical organisation with their African brethren, except that the skull is smaller and the lips thinner—the other a fine, bold, athletic race, with complexions as light as the Spaniards of the south, and little of the usual negro characteristics in their features—faithful, affectionate, and grateful if kindly treated, but turbulent, passionate, and revengeful when smarting under a sense of injury; Mozambiques, short, broad-chested, and muscular, with features expressive of coarse sensuality, and indifference to everything save the gratification of their immediate wants; and here and there an Abyssinian, tall, erect, and handsome, with aquiline features, approaching nearer to the European type than those of any other of the dark races of Africa. Besides the Hindoos, he sees other stray specimens of the Asiatic races: Lascar seamen, with round caps, and cotton petticoats, resembling in shape a Highlander's kilt, worn over the trousers; Batavians, dwarfish, but muscular, with features a compromise between the Hindoo and the Chinese; Armenians, with bushy black beards, and olive complexions, wearing conical caps of sheepskin, with the wool worn outside; Cingalese, differing little, but still discernible, from the Hindoos; and Parsees, from Bombay, fair, sleek, and intelligent, with flowing robes of snowy white, and conical caps reclining rather than worn on the back of the head—a fine race, the mercantile aristocracy of India and the East.

Europe also has added its contingent to swell the motley assembly : bronzed Frenchmen, with a forest of hair about their faces, and a frequent *sacré* on their lips ; stray specimens of Italian and German patriots, exiles for their country's good ; English merchants, principally " old salters," that have exchanged the log-book for the ledger, tropical Trunnions, with many oddities and much warmth of heart—officers and soldiers, looking wan and dissipated, often consciously killing themselves with hard living, and caring little how soon the goal is reached—and last, but not least, the heads of civil departments, grave men, impressed with a sense of their own importance, having an air of greater wisdom than is ever given to mortal man to possess, bearing the burden of the State upon their shoulders, and conscious of its weight.   Other stray waifs of humanity complete the picture, the effect of which is still more heightened by the mixture of Creoles, composing the coloured population, with more or less of African blood in their viens—a distinct class, forming a sort of *imperium in imperio*, equally removed from the pure black and white population, with whom they neither marry nor are given in marriage.

Such is the picture presented to the eye by the mixed and motley population of Mauritius—a picture unique in itself, such as no other country in the world can supply.   There is a great problem being gradually solved by the intermixture of these races, differing so widely in every respect, and what language or man shall emerge from the seething mass, it is difficult to say. We are certain, that the future language of Mauritius will puzzle the philologists of coming ages, and that it will require more than the lingual acquirements of an Admirable Crichton, or of the Italian cardinal * who spoke twenty-four languages, to trace its component parts to the sources from which they were derived. In after ages it may afford an argument in proof of all languages having been derived from one *stamm-sprache*, or mother-tongue, inasmuch as it will be found to have taxed almost all languages in its own composition. But who the " coming man " of Mauritius may be, we cannot tell; we only hope that from elements so diverse, there may not come forth a Frankenstein. One thing is certain, that the Asiatics, the Africans, and the people of colour, are increasing so rapidly as to make the white French population comparatively insignificant in point of numbers; and as a large proportion of the latter are labouring under conditions unfavourable to the propagation of the human race, it is not improbable that in the course of time they may die out, or be absorbed in the coloured population. The latter are rapidly increasing in numbers and wealth, while the white descendants of the original settlers have, in many cases, sunk into poverty. It has been calculated that three-fourths of the immoveable property in the colony is now in possession of the coloured people, and the cause of this transference is to be found in the social habits of the colonists.

* Mezzofanti.

The negresses appear to have always had stronger
attractions for them than the females of their own race
and colour, and as soon as the passions begin to manifest themselves in the young men, connexions are
formed which result in increasing the coloured population. Often these connexions are only dissolved by
death, and both parties are as faithful to each other as
if they were united by the marriage vow. The men
who form these ties are rarely looked upon with
favour by the better class of their own countrywomen, who can scarcely be expected to accept with
pleasure the place in their hearts and homes formerly occupied by a race whom they despise. Thus
they are content (to use the local phrase) to live and
to die *comme ça même,* and after death they bequeath their property and their name to their coloured offspring. It is in this way, principally, that
the gradual transference of property has been effected,
and so general and widely spread are the connexions to
which we allude, that it is probable that in the course
of a century or two, the white population will be
absorbed by the coloured, or that the few remaining
descendants of the former lords of the soil will become
the servants of a class whom they detest. The prospect
of this coming change is sometimes gloated over with
savage pleasure by the organ of the coloured people;
and should the day ever come, there will be a fearful
reckoning for long years of oppression, hatred, and
ridicule. It must be admitted, that by their servile
imitation of their former masters, in dress, manners,

and social intercourse, and the failures necessitated by the unfavourable position in which they are placed, they too often expose themselves to the shafts of ridicule, with which their adversaries are ever ready to wound their vanity. The latter, instead of trying to improve their manners, or affording them an opportunity of attaining that refinement, the absence of which forms the subject of their ridicule, carefully debar them from their *salons*, and *taboo* them as unworthy of their notice. This social ostracism is keenly felt and resented, and the gratuitous insults heaped upon them by the organ of the old French party, have sunk deep into the hearts and memories of a race remarkable for vanity, and ambitious of social equality. Recently they were consoled by the promise held out in the print to which we allude— "Lorsque vous aurez appris le jargon social, vous aurez l'entrée des salons."* This promise implied, of course, that at the present moment they were a set of savages, ignorant even of the language employed in the social intercourse of refined society. It is such insults as these that widen the breach between two classes that speak the same language, and have much of the same blood in their veins, and that would inevitably bring on a civil war, were there not enough of British bayonets and British batons to preserve peace.

The wharf at the landing-place is surrounded by boats of a large size, used for conveying the sugar to the

* " When you have learned the language of society, you will be admitted into our drawing-rooms."

ships. The sugar is contained in bags manufactured from the leaf of the vacouas (*pandanus utilis*), found in abundance in the neighbouring island of Madagascar, and also in Mauritius. The usual quantity contained in these bags is about one hundred and fifty pounds. When a planter has sugar to dispose of, he sends a specimen to his broker in Port Louis, who submits it to the inspection of the different merchants, and sells it at the current price. These brokers form a very flourishing community; and as they generally dabble a little in bills, and are not averse to usury, the most of them are comparatively wealthy. If there should be no demand for sugar, or if the broker thinks that a rise will soon take place, the sugar is stowed away in large stores built for the purpose near the harbour. The planter may be in want of money, and to raise the sum which he requires he has recourse to what are called *dock-warrants*. He obtains a document signed by the keeper of the store to the effect that he has so much sugar in his keeping, and through this document he tries to raise the money. To make the honesty of the storekeepers doubly sure, and to prevent fraud, every one, on entering upon this business, is bound to find sureties to the amount of two thousand pounds, which sum may be forfeited. Such a system is liable to many objections, and there can be no doubt but that money is often raised on fictitious dock-warrants. A striking proof of this recently occurred. A man of the name of B—— kept a large sugar store. His character stood high, and many poor people, tempted by the high rate of interest which he offered, entrusted their small savings to his keeping. He formed the acquaintance of one M——, a sugar broker. M—— being in want of money, persuaded B—— to sign a fictitious dock-warrant. B—— consented, on the condition that a similar application should never be made to him again, to which condition M—— promised faithfully to adhere. Soon after, M—— applied for the same favour. B——, fearful of detection, reminded him of his promise, and declined. M——, who seems to have been a sort of Mauritian Mephistopheles, coolly remarked that he was in his power, and that if he made any difficulty about obliging him, he would at once denounce him to the authorities. We know not whether B——'s feelings corresponded with those ascribed by Goethe to Faust—

> " A good man in the direful grasp of ill,
> The consciousness of right retaineth still."

Possibly he was not a good man. If he was, and retained " the consciousness of right," it had very little practical influence on his conduct. *Facilis descensus averni:* he sunk deeper and deeper, till discovery became inevitable. To escape the consequences, the two associates in crime embarked on board a small vessel belonging to one of them, taking with them the fruits of their dishonesty, and set sail for Madagascar. B—— left a letter, addressed to one of his dupes, in which he acknowledged his guilt, and declared M—— to have been his evil genius. So, doubtless, he had; but it is written in a book which B—— and his compatriots affect very much to despise, that if we resist the devil he will flee from us. He failed to resist the first approach of evil, and therefore he fell. A small vessel, with an officer of justice and a few constables, was sent in pursuit. They discovered the *Joker* at Madagascar, and took possession of her. They found on board a considerable quantity of gold, and M—— labouring under an attack of fever. B—— had been left on shore. They landed, and were proceeding to apprehend him, when he appealed to the Hovas, reminding them that the British would not allow them to seize their fugitives when they reached Mauritius. The appeal was successful; and the officer of police was obliged to return without his prey. It was afterwards reported that they were dead, but this is doubtful. After some years they may yet return in safety to Mauritius, where successful roguery is sure to meet with a large share of sympathy and admiration.

On landing at the wharf, the stranger finds it crowded with Coolies carrying the sugar from the sheds to the boats which convey it to the ships. He cannot but be struck with the miserable appearance and melancholy expression of those poor immigrants. They look as if a smile had never visited their dreary countenances, and the effect of their woeful visages is heightened by the dull monotonous chant with which they accompany their labours. The sight of these half-naked savages does not produce a pleasing impression, and it is felt that civilisation, with its many blessings, has failed as yet to extend to them its humanising influences.

On landing, there are none of those convenient appendages to hotels, known as " touters," to receive the traveller with eager offers of hospitality, and to laud the superior advantages of their respective establishments. It may be the effect of modesty, or of a deep-rooted confidence in their own merits, but the landlords of Mauritius have not yet attained to the dignity of " touters." They think, perhaps, that as good wine requires no bush, a good house should stand on its own merits; and while prepared to receive all comers, they despise to do as their brother Bonifaces in Europe—to send forth to the highways and the harbours in search of travellers. This assumption of dignity, which extends to all the different classes of tradesmen, is extremely inconvenient to the traveller who lands beneath the scorching rays of a vertical sun, amid clouds of dust and the jabbering of unknown tongues. He finds a negro basking in the sun, enjoying the highest amount of happiness of which the African imagination can conceive—the *dolce far' niénte.* Knowing that he is in a British colony, and addressing a British subject, he points to his carpet-bag, and requests to have it carried to a hotel. The British subject rolls his eyes in a manner that must try the powers of tension of the optic nerve, and answers with a grin, " N'a pas connè l'Anglais."* Faintly remembering that this colony some fifty years ago was in the possession of France, he is astonished to find even one inhabitant retaining an imperfect recollection

* " Don't know English."

of the French language, and looks upon him as a sort
of fossil remain of an extinct nationality. He addresses
himself to a second, a third, a fourth, and receives the
same invariable answer, "N'a pas connè l'Anglais."
He looks in vain for an Englishman; they seem as
rare, or more so, than black swans. He addresses himself to the Coolies, British subjects *à double titre*, and
is answered with a "Main nahin junta"* by the more
recent arrivals; by the old immigrants, with the ever-
recurring "N'a pas connè," varied by all the harmonies
of oriental articulation. Astonished and disappointed,
he is disposed to soliloquise, if the sun would permit,
and to say, What! Is it possible that the English
language is unknown to all save Englishmen, in a
colony which has been in the possession of England
since 1810? Is it credible that the Coolies even are
taught the barbarous jargon known as Creole, and
that an Englishman, standing in an English colony,
should discern no traces of the English language, of
English manners, and of English civilisation? And
yet can it be true that the inhabitants of this colony, accustomed under their former Governors to
the strictness of military despotism, and knowing
under the present system nothing of that moral and
religious training which alone can fit men for the
enjoyment of rational liberty, divided by colour and
caste into two great factions, which would inevitably cut one another's throats, if British bayonets did
not intervene, and ignoring English institutions and

* "I do not know."

manners, save for the purpose of holding them up to ridicule and scorn—that the Mauritians, in short (to those who know them the name expresses much), are anxious to obtain the political rights freely and happily accorded to other British colonies, and that the Home Government has shewn certain symptoms of a desire to gratify their wishes? Earl Grey's theory of gradually accustoming the colonies to the exercise of political rights, till they are fit for emancipation from the mother-country, can scarcely apply to an island where, apart from the military, not more than a thousand of the two hundred and thirty thousand inhabitants can speak English, or identify themselves with England as their mother-country. If he knew, further, that trial by jury, and the Municipal Council of Port Louis, have, to use a local phrase, *functioned* in such a manner as to cover these institutions with deserved ridicule and contempt, he would hesitate which to admire most, the audacity of the popular demagogues in clamouring for institutions of which they scarcely know the names, or the weakness of the Home Government in yielding, in any measure, to claims, the recognition of which would distract the colony with intestine broils, and lead to endless confusion. A more enlarged experience would lead him to the conclusion, that a pure despotism, mildly but firmly exercised, is the form of government best adapted to this colony, and that the attempt to engraft free institutions, the gradual growth of centuries, upon a people descended from slaves and slaveholders, that are still

smarting under the remembrance of the lash, or long-
ing to resume it, can only lead to failure and disappointment.

These remarks must be regarded as the fruit of our
traveller's after-experience. We have left him standing
soliloquising on the wharf at Port Louis. The heat of
the sun leads him for the nonce to think of other
matters. He is sick of salt junk and similar dainties,
and anxious to take his ease in his inn, if he can only
find it. Making a virtue of necessity, he strings
together the few words of French still remaining in
the storehouse of his memory. Fortunately his audience are not critical, and the exhibition of his purse
awakens the intelligence of one of those hideous
negroes that are always lounging about the wharf and
the bazaar. With some misgivings he consigns his
carpet-bag to his care, and orders him to look out for
a carriage. He conducts him past the Custom-house,
a large white building opposite the wharf. He threads
his way through loaded Coolies, mules, and sugar-carts,
till he reaches the open space, where there is a clump
of ship-chandlers' shops. He passes these, turns the
corner, and reaches the square known as the Place
d'Armes. On the right-hand side, as he advances, is
the military guard-room, the office of the Commissariat,
and Godon's Symposium, where gods, sable as Pluto,
indulge in nectar and ambrosia. On the left are the
Exchange Rooms, where merchants most do congregate,
and seat themselves, or recline, like Tityrus, beneath
the shade of the far-spreading beech or tamarind tree

—" *tenui meditantes avena* " — meditating on the
growth and price of the sugar-cane.   Some of these,
like honest Dogberry, have had losses in their day, and
found their claims to respect mainly on that circumstance.   Others would have lost their all, had it not
been found when the day of reckoning came, that, with
a generosity which forms an admirable feature in the
character of Mauritius husbands, they had previously
settled their all on their wives, from whose gentle but
tenacious grasp no avaricious creditors could wrest it.
Shrewd men these merchants of the Place—cunning in
all manner of devices connected with the sugar market
—having a keen eye to the main chance—and hailing
often from the Land of Cakes and the canny capital of
the West.   They form the most intelligent and best
educated class in the colony—are hospitable, warm-
hearted, and generous—and though not remarkable for
their religious tendencies, ready to support every charitable and religious institution.   Few of them, however,
are wealthy, and the wealth of the wealthy few would
appear insignificant beside the colossal fortunes of
some of the merchant princes of England.   Few of
these can be regarded as permanent residents in the
colony.   Their object is to make a certain sum of
money, and when that object is attained, they betake
themselves to other lands, where money is more valuable and life more enjoyable than in Mauritius.

The traveller, standing on the Place, and anxious to
find a vehicle to convey him to his hotel, finds that he has
arrived at the right place.   He sees himself surrounded

with vehicles of all kinds, from the rude *carriole*, with its active and spirited pony, to the luxurious carriage of Jones, with its elastic cushions, and dashing grays from the Cape. He is hailed by the title of captain, in broken English or in pure Hindustanee, by the different charioteers, who appear to have sacrificed little to the graces, and to have made a narrow escape from being downright savages. The better class of carriages are driven by Creoles, remarkable for reckless driving, and that insolence and readiness to overreach which seems to characterise the cabmen of all countries. They sit at ease upon their boxes, smoking short black pipes or cheap cigars, and wearing old hats that seem previously to have decorated the head of some antiquated scarecrow. They have a remarkable facility in distinguishing among the passengers those who are likely to become their fares, and address them in such terms as they think will be most flattering to their self-love. The fare for a single person is one shilling to any place within the bounds of the municipality, and this sum, compared with other charges, must be regarded as very moderate. There are nearly three hundred carrioles, or small spring-carts, on the Place, drawn by powerful little ponies from Timor or Pegu, and driven by the proprietors, who are usually Indians that have saved a little money and embarked it in this speculation. The space which these hardy little creatures can traverse in the course of a day, with the carrioles loaded with three or four passengers, is something incredible. The distance from Port Louis to the Savanne is about

thirty miles, and yet a Pegu pony has been known to
make the journey and to return in the same day.
Fortunately for their proprietors, there is no society
for the suppression of cruelty to animals in Mauritius,
otherwise these useful animals might meet with better
treatment. If the traveller is troubled with indigestion,
a short drive in a carriole may have a good effect, provided always that his nerves are in a healthy condition,
and that he sets no overdue value on the preservation
of his life or the safety of his limbs. The driver
makes him clamber up into the ricketty vehicle in the
best way he can, and seats him behind himself. His
head is protected from the rays of a vertical sun by a
rough canopy of wood or tin, supported on iron rods
attached to the framework of the carriole, and his
person is concealed from the gaze of the *profanum
vulgus* by a species of cotton curtains that have once
been whiter and cleaner. The driver usually wears a
species of head-dress, that forms a sort of compromise
between a *bonnet rouge* and a Kilmarnock night-cap.
He abjures the use of a whip, but uses in lieu a large
leather strap, which he wields with a dexterity that
might excite the envy of a hedge schoolmaster. The
traveller finds that with carrioles, as with many other
things, *ce n'est que le premier pas qui coûte*. The
poor little brute, knowing what is in store for him, is
shy of starting, and plunges and rears, till, overpowered
by the lashes that are showered upon him, and the un-
earthly yells of his savage driver, he at length rushes
forward. The noise is indescribable. The canopy

shakes, the curtains flap, the iron rods rattle, the
springs grate, and the wheels, innocent of oil, creak as
if the whole affair were going to pieces. Coachmen and
riders with restive horses give the carriole as wide a
berth as the poet bestows on Gilpin. The traveller is
suffocated with dust and stupified with noise. In vain
he appeals to his goblin-like driver, who is now in his
element. His enthusiasm reaches its climax at the
sound of a rival carriole approaching. His eye lightens
up

> " With that strange joy which warriors feel
> In foemen worthy of their steel,"

and on he drives with the reckless rapidity of the
spectre horseman in Leonore, till he reaches his goal,
or overturns his vehicle, in either of which cases he is
equally unmoved, and if a Mohammedan, acknowledges
the greatness of Allah with pious resignation.

The carriole is a luxury to be enjoyed at an after
period, and the traveller on first landing had better
imitate our example, and drive in a comfortable carriage to the Hotel de l'Europe.

The taste of the Creoles for gay colours is shewn in
the painting of their carriages. An Englishman associates the quietest colours in dress and equipage with
respectability—a Creole judges of these matters by a
different standard. The carriages on the Place shew
the richness of his imagination by the splendour and
variety of the colours which the painter's brush has
bestowed upon them. A tartan of the Royal Stuart
pattern seems to predominate, while a bright blue is

the next favourite colour. The most of these carriages
belong to men of colour, and the fertility of the African
imagination has been taxed in the selection of new and
startling colours. When the perfect *enfranchisement*
of the African race has been effected, it will be accompanied with a new civilisation, and an original application of the arts to the production of new forms that
will startle our sober northern ideas of the beautiful
and the becoming.

At the top of the Place stands Government House,
a large inelegant building, forming three sides of
a square, with the open space facing the harbour.
The ground-floor, built under the direction of La
Bourdonnais, is composed of coral. At the capture
of the island in 1810, the building was in an un-
finished state, and though completed, it cannot be said
to have been improved by the subsequent governors.
It consists of three storeys, with corresponding veran-
dahs, and the public rooms in the centre storey are
large and handsome, with polished floors—beautiful to
look at, but dangerous to the equilibrium of the uninitiated. The offices of the Governor's staff are
situated in the lowest storey, and the uppermost is
composed of sleeping apartments. In front there is a
paved court-yard, with a flagstaff. The hoisting of
the national colours indicates the presence of her
Majesty's representative. In the hot season, the flag
generally remains unfurled, except on Wednesdays,
when the Council meets. The cool retreats and shady
alleys of Reduit, with its European temperature and

beautiful cascade, have far greater attractions than the stifling atmosphere of this huge barn. The sooner it is sold to the Town Council, who are anxious to instal themselves in its lofty apartments, and whose salamander constitutions can stand any amount of heat, the more creditable it will be to the representative of Majesty in Mauritius. A Government House worthy of the name will then be erected, and form one of the very few public buildings in this town that have any claims to architectural beauty.

To the left of Government House is Royal Street; to the right the Chaussée. The first of these is a fine large street, composed of houses built almost entirely of stone, and used principally as shops or stores. The Chaussée is narrower and closer, and most of the houses are built of wood. Wood is less used for building purposes since 1816, when a considerable portion of the town was consumed by fire. To the right of Government House, with the entrance from Royal Street, are the offices of the Chief Medical Officer and of the Colonial Secretary, situated in a long narrow building, with a stifling atmosphere, and a shabbiness of appearance reflecting little credit on the Government that allows it to be used for such a purpose. To the left of Government House, facing Government Street, are the offices of the Auditor-General, the Treasurer, and the Postmaster—buildings erected on the strictest principles of economy, and exactly similar in character to the one already described.

In ascending Government Street, after passing Government House, the first large building to the right is the Ice-house, the most popular establishment in Port Louis during the hot season. To the left is the Theatre, a large unwieldy building, not unlike Government House in its general cumbrousness of appearance. Around it may be seen groups of slim youths, dressed in exaggerated imitation of the most recent Parisian fashions, as displayed in the coloured prints in the tailors' windows, smoking cigars manufactured in the colony, and sold at the moderate charge of one halfpenny each, discussing with all the airs of accomplished *dilettánti* the appearance of the *prima donna* in the opera of the previous evening. These are the *jeunes gens*— the rising generation of Mauritius.

A few yards beyond the theatre, on the right-hand side, is the Hotel de l'Europe; but let the traveller weigh well the contents of his purse before he enters its inviting gate. If his appetite be craving and his purse slender, let him betake himself to some more humble hostelry, where he may eat and be satisfied, without ruining himself in the process. If he fail to adopt our advice, he will have reason to repent his audacity when the landlord refreshes his memory with his little *mémoire*. Occasionally a reckless subaltern on his way to India has been reminded of the appositeness of the inscription which Dante saw over the entrance of a certain place, and tempted to apply it to the place of his temporary incarceration—

" Lasciate ogni speránza, voi ch'entrate,"

as he waits for remittances that do *not* come, and eats

dinners which, to borrow a French idiom, he must some day pay through the nose, or break the *parole* on which his landlord has placed him. A private dinner at the Hotel de l'Europe costs more than the same meal at the Clarendon ; and if the traveller is accompanied by his wife we should scarcely advise him to dine at the table d'hôte. There is a freedom in the conversation such as would never be sanctioned in any similar establishment on the Continent, and an occasional mixture of *gros sel*, tickling enough to the palates of its Creole frequenters, but scarcely adapted to the tastes of our British wives and sisters. If the traveller meditates a brief sojourn, and finds his purse in a satisfactory condition, he may enter. On crossing the threshold, he finds himself in a large hall, floored with marble, and filled with half-naked servants disputing among themselves in Creole, and shewing little alacrity in attending to his wants. The walls are covered with paper, on which are represented landscapes, in that style of art which was so much in vogue in the reign of Louis XV. The stairs and floors of the upper rooms are composed of wood, and rubbed with wax till they are dazzlingly bright and dangerously slippery. The bed-rooms are small, and so ill ventilated that in the hot season sleeping with the windows shut is impossible. The beds are composed of iron bars that have been once gilt, and covered with muslin curtains to admit the air and keep out the mosquitoes. The furniture is of the simplest description. It consists of a cane-bottomed chair and a small wooden table, both of which have seen service. If he finds a mirror, the traveller may esteem himself fortunate. Fire-place there is none, nor is it required. A thin pannel partition separates him from his next neighbour. If the latter has eaten a heavy dinner, or is at all of an apoplectic tendency, he will be fully apprised of that fact.

For the use of this bed-room, with breakfast at nine o'clock, and dinner at the table d'hôte at six, the traveller pays six dollars (twenty-four shillings). The principal dish at breakfast is curry, and the favourite beverage claret and water. The dinner consists of several *entrées*, and the different dishes are cooked in the French style. The soup and the salad are good, the other dishes too highly seasoned, or too greasy, to please the palate before it is accustomed to Creole cookery. Immediately after dinner, coffee is served in small cups, with the usual accompaniment of a *petit verre* of brandy. The guests then disperse, and the regular frequenters of the house seat themselves in the verandah to enjoy the coolness of the evening air and the soothing influences of the cigar. The smallness of the space, within which their lives are circumscribed, does not leave room for much variety in the conversation of the Creoles. The ship captains discuss the merits of their vessels, the character of their agents, and the freights at the different places they have visited. The Frenchmen, whom the hope of fortune has enticed to this little spot in the Indian Ocean, declare life to be very *triste*, and long for the cafés, the theatres, and the gaieties of Paris. While six dollars is the nominal sum which the traveller pays for the conveniences we have enumerated, if he thinks that that amount will cover all his expenses he will soon find that he has reckoned without his host. The latter personage has a most retentive memory for the smallest offices that have been rendered beneath his roof, and an extravagant idea of their value. To escape this unexpected drain upon his purse, the traveller should in every case make a bargain with the landlord for a fixed sum. This is the usual practice, and ought never to be neglected.

There are two other hotels in Port Louis, occasionally frequented by travellers—Masse's Hotel, near the Chaussée, and George's Hotel, behind the theatre. The former is an old establishment, and while it is less central and attractive than the Hotel de l'Europe, the landlord has the reputation of being the best cook in the colony., His charge for the same accommodation as at the Europe Hotel is four dollars, instead of six. George's Hotel partakes more of the character of a private boarding-house than of a regular hotel. Its rooms are generally occupied by permanent residenters in the colony, and a friend of mine who lived there six months, speaks in favourable terms of the landlord, who is a coloured man.

Before dismissing the Mauritius landlords, a word must be said in their favour. The traveller, before condemning in too strong terms their apparently extravagant charges, must take into account their peculiar position, which resembles that of the hotel-keepers on any of the great routes in Europe, whose houses are frequented by travellers only during a few months of the year, and remain almost without a guest till the next season brings its tide of visitors. The establishment must be kept up throughout the year, and the travellers, though not using it, must pay for its support. The Mauritius land-lords, also, pay an exorbitant sum as house-rent, and their expenditure, in a colony where all the necessaries of life are imported at a high rate, must be very great. There is this difference, also, between their position and that of their brother Bonifaces in Europe, that while travellers must patronise the latter, the former are cheated of their lawful prey by the hospitable English residents who are ever ready to open their kind homes for the reception of all who have any claims upon their attention. No wonder, then, that the landlords of Mauritius, when they catch any unfortunate traveller, do their utmost *pour faire valoir le bouchon.*

It happened to be a Sunday morning when I landed in Mauritius. Every traveller fresh from England, who lands on the same day, will speedily be reminded that this colony, though nominally English, is essentially French in all its habits and customs. He will find open canteens and arrack-shops, less gorgeous than the gin-palaces of London, but doing their work with the same deadly effect. He will be jostled by gangs of drunken sailors spending their Sunday ashore, and imparting to the heathen Coolie from Hindostan his first ideas of the Christian character. If he pass near the bazaar, he will have to thread his way among groups of Indians that have been long enough in the colony to profit by their Christian brother's example, and to imbibe a taste for the poison sold in the canteens. He will meet vehicles of all kinds, from the luxurious carriage to the rattling carriole, filled with the citizens of the better class, hurrying to the country to spend the Sabbath at Pamplemousses. He will find the shops open, and their goods exposed for sale; the bazaar thronged by busy purchasers ; and every place of public resort attracting its share of attention, save the house of God, the visitors to which seem to be few and far between. He will hear the clang of the blacksmith's hammer, and all the other sounds of labour that are hushed and silent on an English Sabbath; and if it be the sugar season, and prices are rising, he will see the smoke ascending from the mills, and the bands of Coolies cutting down the canes in the fields. At first, he may flatter himself that Sabbath labour is confined to the French Creoles. This delusion will speedily vanish. He will soon find that the English engineer and the English planter, who, when they return home, will perhaps join societies for enforcing the better observance of the Sabbath, are as ready to labour on the Sabbath as their Creole neighbours. One or two fearful accidents—or, shall we say judgments?—that have overtaken Englishmen labouring on the Sabbath, may deter their fellow-planters for a time from working their machinery on that sacred day, but a sudden rise in the sugar market, or the dread of an unfavourable season, is sufficient to make them return to their former course. What will not the lust of gold effect? We speak of these men as a class. Among the English residents in Mauritius there are as good and consistent Christians as are to be found at home, but their name is not legion. They are not many.

After you have been " cribb'd, cabin'd, and confined " in a merchant ship for nearly four months, and fed upon salt provisions, the first breakfast on shore is a luxury to be remembered in after years with a feeling of lively satisfaction. The hard musty biscuit—in its best estate a miserable substitute for bread—is exchanged for the delicate French roll, fresh butter, tea and coffee with cream; and the pleasant variety of tropical fruits, though enjoyable at all seasons, have a delightful zest when partaken of for the first time after a long voyage. You feel that the pleasures of the first meal ashore almost compensate for the privations of the past voyage, and astonish the Creole waiter by the rapidity with which you despatch the good things spread out for your refreshment.

An officer on the staff opened his hospitable home for my reception till I had made arrangements about my future movements. I accompanied him in the forenoon to the English church, situated in La-Bourdonnais Street, in the neighbourhood of the Champ de Mars. The building now used as a church was originally a powder magazine. To judge from the frigid manner in which the whole service was conducted, one might have been tempted to believe that the building was still filled with some combustible material, which it required the strictest caution to prevent from exploding. Owing to some defect in his organs of speech, the officiating minister's voice was inaudible even to those seated nearest to the pulpit, and the empty pews shewed that the English Protestants in Mauritius were indeed to be pitied as *habitantes in sicco*. All this has now been changed. The present English bishop is an eloquent preacher, a laborious and devoted pastor, full of a missionary spirit, and ready to assist in every good work. Although his unceasing labours cannot raise Protestantism to the position which, if fairly represented at first, it ought to have occupied in this colony, they have already effected a great change in the attendance at church. Every pew is now occupied, and it is pleasing to observe that the poor as well as the rich meet at the house of God to hear the glad tidings of salvation through Him, who, while He was rich, yet for our sakes became poor, that we, through His poverty, might be made rich.

I accompanied my friend in the afternoon to an Independent chapel, where the congregation is composed of Creoles, and the service conducted in French. It is a low-roofed building, situated behind the civil prison, and capable of containing about four hundred worshippers. On approaching it, I was rather astonished at seeing a number of coloured lads lounging about the door and smoking cigars, as if it had been the entrance to a theatre. The congregation amounted to about a hundred persons, principally young negresses and women of colour. Their dress was generally composed of white muslin. Few of them wore shoes or stockings. The younger females had their heads uncovered, while the more elderly wore Madras handkerchiefs of rather a gay pattern, rolled turban-fashion round the head. The singing seemed to be the part of the service in which they felt most interested. The prayers and sermon were listened to with respectful but half-drowsy attention. When the singing came, the rich dark African eye was lighted up with enthusiastic feeling, and the different hymns were sung with great power and considerable skill, which shewed that the performers had been carefully trained. The missionary who officiated was a young man, a son of the Rev. J. Lebrun, who has devoted nearly forty years to the work of evangelising the African race in the Mauritius, and who, after surmounting many difficulties, can point to four Protestant congregations in different parts of the island as the fruit of his labours.

We attended the evening service at the English church. There were not twenty persons in the whole church. The service was conducted by the Rev. L. Banks, a kind, warm-hearted Irishman, who, if properly supported, might have effected much good in the colony, but whose usefulness was marred by causes on which it is not necessary to enter. He imbibed the seeds of disease, during his unremitting attention to the sick, in the fearful outbreak of cholera with which this island was visited in 1854, and died—where the soldier of the Cross should die—in the field of duty. A handsome marble tablet, with an appropriate inscription, has been erected to his memory in the interior of the church. Peace to his ashes! He was a good man, full of the Holy Ghost and of faith.

CHAPTER II.

Scarcity of Houses in Port Louis—Hospitality—Pamplemousses Gardens
—Paul and Virginia—Their Monuments—Dearness of Living—
Traditional Furniture—Chinamen—Origin of Slavery—Execution of
a Dutch Slave—Ruling Passion Strong at Death—First French
Colonists—La Bourdonnais—The Slave Trade—Romantic Incident
—Abolition of Slavery by the French Republicans—Re-established by
Napoleon—Slavery under the British Government—Treatment of
Slaves by the French—St Pierre—Sonnerat—Baron Grant—Harrow-
ing Sufferings of the Slaves—The Code Noir—Cruelty of Female
Slaveholders—State of Crime among the Slaves—Marriage and its
Punishment—Superstition—Language, Specimen of—Emancipation
of the Slaves—Its Consequences—Present Condition of the Ex-slave
Population and their Descendants.

A STRANGER, about to take up his residence permanently
in Mauritius, usually finds some difficulty in obtaining
a suitable house. The population of Port Louis has
increased very much of late years, but few new houses
have been built, as the inhabitants have found better
investments for their money. In consequence of this,
a stranger is often obliged to wait till the departure of
some English or French resident for Europe enables
him to obtain a lease of his house. A highly respected
merchant, himself " a kindly Scot," received me into
his hospitable house, and entertained me for two
months, till I was able to secure a house in town. It
was amusing to observe the hold which old Scottish
associations had over his mind, after many years of

absence, and the outward expression which they assumed.
His comfortable bungalow was known as Burnside
House, and his butler rejoiced in the name of Dugald.
Many a poor missionary, on his way home from India,
retains a grateful remembrance of his generous kindness and warm-hearted hospitality. A short time before
my arrival, a vessel from Ceylon put in at Port Louis
for repairs, which detained her three months. During
that time a missionary, his wife, and three children,
who were obliged to leave the ship, were kindly entertained by the owner of Burnside House, to whom they
were perfect strangers.

Accompanied by my kind host's obliging nephew, I
visited the Botanical Gardens at Pamplemousses, the
great place of resort for passing visitors. While the
term botanical is rather misapplied to these gardens, they
are interesting from the collection of trees, shrubs, and
herbaceous plants, peculiar to the tropics, which they
contain. Among the plants are some magnificent sago
palms, and an interesting collection of spice-growing
trees and shrubs. The nutmeg tree is generally an object
of great interest to travellers. Its fruit resembles a
Green Chissel pear, and when it is ripe, it bursts open
and exposes to view the nutmeg, covered with its coating
of bright red mace. Mr Duncan, the kind and obliging
gardener, is ever ready to supply travellers with specimens of the nutmeg, which, when preserved in brine,
fórm an interesting souvenir of Mauritius. A specimen
of the mangoustan tree, the fruit of which is regarded
as superior to every other, may also be seen; but owing

to the difference of soil and climate between Mauritius and Malacca, from which it was brought, the fruit never reaches maturity. Mr Duncan has made an extensive collection of the ferns indigenous to the island, and the traveller will never regret a day spent amid the fine shady alleys and tropical exuberance of Pamplemousses Gardens.

To the sentimentalist the loveliest productions of nature are less attractive than the most common objects that are in any way associated with the productions of genius. The pen of Bernardin St Pierre has done more to attract the traveller to Pamplemousses, than the rarest productions of the tropics, and the monuments of Paul and Virginia, simple pedestals of clay, surmounted with urns, have excited more admiration than the far-famed traveller's tree. Whoever wishes to have before his mind's eye a faithful and comprehensive picture of the natural scenery of the island, should read St Pierre's charming work, which could only have been written by one who had a thorough sympathy with nature, and a keen appreciation of her beauties. It is a painful task at all times to unwind the web of fair romance which the hand of genius has spun, and to analyse the material of which each thread is composed. If St Pierre's tale were subjected to this test, it would stand the ordeal better than most other works of the same character. There is an air of reality throughout the whole work, which owes but little to the author's imagination. His fancy may have filled up the minor details, but the outline of the work is founded

on reality. I have read over the deposition of the five
sailors who survived the wreck of the *St Gèran*. The
vessel seems to have been lost through the ignorance
and obstinacy of the officer in command. A common
sailor, who knew the coast, ventured to remonstrate
with this officer, and was answered with a blow. Soon
after the vessel struck. There was a young lady on
board, the daughter of a planter, who was returning
from France, where she had been sent for her education. A young officer had become enamoured of her
during the voyage, and was anxious to save her life.
The scene described by St Pierre was actually witnessed
by the spectators on shore, and among others by the
young lady's father, who could render no assistance :—

> " The waters wild went o'er his child,
> And he was left lamenting."

From the sublime to the ridiculous, from Paul and
Virginia, painted by St Pierre, to their monuments at
Pamplemousses, there is only a step. These monuments have been erected from a wish to gratify the
desire which the mind has to give a visible and
tangible reality to the pictures of the imagination. A
distinguished nobleman, Governor-General of India, on
his way to Europe, touched at Mauritius, and dined at
Government House. The conversation chanced upon
Paul and Virginia, when the Indian guest asked if
there was no tomb to mark the grave of the heroine.
The Mauritius Governor was about to answer in the
negative, when his aide-de-camp anticipated him with
the reply that there was a monument over the remains

of Virginia, and that he could drive to Pamplemousses and examine it the next day before dinner. The guests belonging to the colony, who knew that the spot where Virginia was interred, far from being marked by any monument, was even unknown, looked rather aghast at this statement, but left the aide-de-camp to justify it as best he might. Next day the Governor-General was gratified with the sight of a monument at Pamplemousses, said to have been erected on the very spot where Virginia was buried after the shipwreck. The apparent recency of its erection was explained by the aide-de-camp remarking that it had been repaired immediately before his Excellency's visit. The work of a day was examined with such feelings of veneration as to shew that even a Governor-General may be mystified. The monument took, and the proprietor netted a handsome sum by exhibiting it to travellers. To render the delusion complete, and to gratify the admirers of Paul, his tomb was placed by the side of Virginia's where it has ever since remained. Both these monuments have frequently been destroyed through that iconoclastic tendency peculiar to the Anglo-Saxon race, which would lead some of them to chip off the nose of the Apollo Belvidere, if they could, in order to prove to their friends at home that they have seen that masterpiece of art. The monuments thus destroyed have been replaced by others, which are as much the monuments of Paul and Virginia as those which preceded them.

At the end of two months, I established myself in a small house in Port Louis. No one can know

how dear living is in this colony till he has tried
the experiment. Visitors from India, with large in-
comes, often hasten their departure for this reason. A
small cottage, with four or five rooms, situated on the
Champ de Mars, or the Champ Delort, fetches a rent
of from £80 to £100 per annum. A colonial chaplain, with £400 a-year, finds it difficult to live on his
salary. A correspondent of the *Times* has been trying
to prove of late that a man may marry and be happy
on £300 a-year. I would not advise any one to make
the experiment in Mauritius. Allow the happy Benedict an additional hundred, and he will not be without
his difficulties. One-fourth of his income is absorbed
by the single item of house rent. He will require a
cook, a coachman, a washerman, a female servant, and
a butler ; their united wages will be more than £100.
About £50 per annum must be set aside for keeping
a horse and carriage—a luxury in England, but a necessity in Mauritius. His daily household expenses
will be at least 6s., or £100 per annum, leaving only
£50 to pay for clothes, medical attendance, charities,
and all possible contingencies. These contingencies in
the course of a year are rather numerous. Does he
break the glass of his watch? A new one costs a dollar.
Does his watch require to be cleaned? The usual charge
is five dollars. Does his servant break the glass globe
which holds his lamp (mine broke two in one year)? He
must pay ten dollars to replace it. Does a Malabar
coachman, stupified with gandia, drive against his carriage (nothing is more common)? He will have to pay

from twenty to forty dollars for repairs. But why enlarge upon these contingencies? They are the dark spectres of every poor man's existence in Mauritius. They come often in very questionable shapes, but no one is proof against them.

When a man takes possession of a house in Mauritius, it is not necessary that he should furnish it in the same style as at home. He furnishes gradually, and as opportunity offers. The furniture is at first often of the simplest description. A table, a few chairs, a bed, and a *batterie de cuisine*, are the first requisites. He can add gradually to his stock at the different sales, which occur when his countrymen leave. There are several of these sales every year. An Englishman's furniture is generally bought by Englishmen. It becomes thus, in a measure, national and traditional; and an old residenter, on returning to the colony, often buys the same article which belonged to him years before. These are generally of Indian or Cingalese manufacture, and ebony, of which most of them are made, is so durable, that many of them become almost hereditary. A few of the merchants have their houses furnished with elegant furniture from London; but these are exceptional cases. Most of them, meditating a removal, are content with the articles which their predecessors used. There are certain articles which families, intending to reside in Mauritius, would do well to bring out with them from England. Among these may be mentioned glass, breakfast and dinner services, and plate. Plated ware is usually preferred to pure silver; the latter is apt to find its way to the Malabar jewellers, who soon transmute it into some other shape. Though clothing is rather expensive, it is not advisable to bring an extensive wardrobe from home. There is an insect, supposed to be the same as the one alluded to in Matt. vi. 20, which finds its way into the best secured *armoire*, and feeds upon its contents. Often on bringing out for some special occasion an English-made coat, the owner is astounded at finding it riddled by this mischievous moth, which thus reads him a practical homily on the vanity of earthly things. A tin box is the best preventive against its inroads. A large stock of shirts is indispensable, for two reasons—those sold in the colony are very bad and very dear; those brought from home are subjected to a treatment which would excite the indignation of any decent English washerwoman. The traveller, when approaching Mauritius by sea, on passing near the mouth of Grand River, is surprised by seeing what appears to be a flock of sheep leaping with short bounds into the air in rapid succession, without changing their position. The truth is, that the mouth of the river is the wash-tub of Mauritius. There the clothes of the people of Port Louis, and of the surrounding country districts, are washed in a truly original and primitive fashion. The washermen, who are usually Indians, known in their own language as *dhobies*, first carry the clothes into the stream, where they rub them over with soap, and soak them in the water. They then carry them to the land, wring them into a knot, and beat them with all their might against a stone. The soaking, rubbing, wringing, and beating are repeated several times. They are then spread out in the sun, and sprinkled with water. By means of this process linen attains a whiteness such as is never witnessed in Europe, but it is at the expense of the material, which is soon worn out.

The small house which I occupied was on a level with the street, and I was obliged to leave the windows open to admit the cool air in the evening. A small crowd of black *gamins* used to watch me at dinner with much interest, to judge from their looks and remarks. I had occasional visits at the same hour from a Chinese shopkeeper from the opposite side of the street. He entered my dining-room with the freedom and ease of one who had the *entrée* of the house, examined the food of the barbarian with the air of a *connaisseur*, opened my cupboard, and inspected my tea-caddy. He generally concluded by inviting me, in broken English and Creole, to visit his store, which, knowing the roguish character of his countrymen, I respectfully declined.

There are about two thousand Chinamen in Port Louis. They are principally small traders from Singapore, and are a frugal, industrious, thrifty race. The pork trade of the colony is in their hands. When they purchase a pig, they conduct it to the slaughter-house in a more expeditious way than by driving. They first bind the four legs together with a cord, and then insert a pole between them, which rests upon the shoulders of two sturdy bearers. To prevent the pig from expressing his disapproval of this treatment, he is thoroughly gagged, and becomes one of the quietest and most tractable animals in existence.

Some of them are market gardeners, and the loads they bear balanced on their shoulders give one a high idea of their physical strength. They are the most skilful thieves in the colony. Some of them effected an entrance into the Commercial Bank, a few years ago, by undermining the building, and succeeded in carrying off a large sum of money without being detected. They are also much addicted to opium and gambling. They have a joss-house situated on the road that leads to the Cemetery. It is not much frequented, and the few idols it contains are treated with little respect. Offerings of rice are presented to them on the great festival days, but the Chinaman shews his tendency to roguery even in the treatment of his gods. If you examine that offering of rice, in the shape of a small mound on the floor of the joss-house, it will be found that there is only an outward coating of rice, while the rest is made up of stones and earth—a proof either that the Chinaman's tendency to roguery is irresistible, or that his ideas of the intelligence of his gods are not very exalted. Their religious worship partakes of that practical character which marks their whole conduct. It seems to consist mainly in eating pork, and drinking innumerable small cups of tea. They are the only race in the colony that seem utterly destitute of all religious susceptibility, and satisfied with a hard, bare materialism. I obtained a hundred copies of the

Chinese Testament from Hong Kong, and endeavoured to dispose of them among the Chinamen. I did not find one who could not read, but the few who desired to have copies seemed to value them merely as articles of merchandise. They have a burial-ground at the Cemetery, separated by a wall from the other departments of the dead. Their graves, which are built of stone, have inscriptions, in perpendicular rows of Chinese characters, setting forth, no doubt, the lineage and virtues of the deceased. The stones, on which these inscriptions are cut out, are inserted into the north end of the graves, and are about two feet high. They are generally of basalt, but sometimes of marble. There is a sort of altar, with a marble tablet let into it, projecting from the neighbouring wall, where candles are burned, and some ceremonies performed by the officiating priest at their funerals. They are not in any sense a demonstrative race. They all dress in the same manner, the ordinary costume being a straw hat, a light blouse, and wide trousers. The usual sign over their shops is a huge red placard, intimating that Warren's blacking is sold there. The Chinamen have faith in Warren, and believe this intimation sufficient.

Before attempting to describe the present condition of society in the colony, or to account for the existence of its mixed and motley population, it is necessary to cast a retrospective glance upon the origin, progress, and final abolition of slavery—an institution which leaves its impress upon the character of the inhabitants of every country where it has existed. The origin of slavery in this and other French colonies situated within the tropics, is candidly stated in the preface to the Code Noir:—"As the heat of these climates, and the temperature of ours, prevent Frenchmen from undertaking so painful a labour as the clearing of the uncultivated lands in these burning countries, it was necessary to supply this want by means of men accustomed to the heat of the sun and the greatest degree of fatigue. Hence the importation of negroes from Africa into our colonies. Hence the necessity of slavery, in order to subject a multitude of powerful men to a small number of Frenchmen transplanted into these islands. It cannot be denied that slavery in this case was dictated by prudence and by the wisest policy. Intended only for the cultivation of our colonies, the same necessity which caused the introduction of slaves continues their existence there, and it was never intended that they should bear their chains into the midst of the mother-country." This statement was drawn up at a period when slavery was universal, and when no man had yet raised his voice to protect the miserable African from a system which "was dictated by prudence and the wisest policy."

Slavery was first introduced into Mauritius by the Dutch, who possessed the island from about the middle of the seventeenth century to the year 1712, and bestowed upon it its present name. Two reasons are assigned for their having abandoned the island—the ravages of rats, which almost literally ate them out of house and home, and the necessity of concentrating all their forces at the Cape of Good Hope, so as to place that colony in a state of defence. Nothing is known of the working of slavery under the Dutch, except from a casual allusion of the Abbé Rochon, and the narrative of Le Guat, a Huguenot refugee, who was imprisoned for some time by the Dutch Governor Diodati. The Abbé, in his "Voyage to Madagascar," thus alludes to slavery in Mauritius:—" Pronis, who had been commissioned to take possession of Madagascar in the name of the King of France, was a man of in-ferior talents. He added to his other malversations that of selling to Vander-Mester, then Governor of Mauritius, the unfortunate Malagashes who were in the service of the settlement; but it excited the islanders to the highest pitch of indignation, when they found that among these slaves, there were sixteen women of the race of Lohariths." From Le Guat's narrative, it would appear that the Dutch were not more humane in the treatment of their slaves than their successors in the island:—" The commandant having been informed that a negro had committed some thefts in his kitchen, condemned him to receive the chastisement connected with that offence, which was very severe. The miserable culprit, alarmed at the sufferings with which he was threatened, took to flight, after having plotted a design with one of his comrades and two negro women to set fire to the fort. They accordingly executed their fatal scheme, but were not so fortunate as to escape; they were shortly taken, when the two men suffered the rack, and the women were hanged. One of these wretched

criminals, it seems, had possessed a most inordinate
passion for play, which predominated on the scaffold
where he was about to suffer a most painful death. He
there entreated with the most earnest solicitation, that
some one of the assistants on this awful occasion might,
as an act of charity, be permitted to throw dice with
him for a few minutes, and that he should then suffer
the sentence of the law without regret. If he had any
secret motive for his conduct, it was known only to
himself ; but, be that as it may, no one was disposed to
be of his party, and he appeared to lament the refusal
more than his fate."   This reckless conduct may
appear to have resulted from some peculiar idiosyncrasy
in the negro character, and many may be disposed to
regard it as a proof of his inferior nature.   To prevent
such a conclusion, and to prove that it is the same
human heart which beats beneath the *pallium* of a cardinal and the rags of a negro, we quote the following
anecdote from " Louis XIV. and his Age." The author
is describing the death-bed of Cardinal Mazarin:—
" Gambling, which had been his ruling passion, survived
all others.   Being no longer able to play himself, he
caused others to play around his bed; being no longer
able to hold the cards, he caused another to hold them
for him.   Play was thus carried on, till the moment
when the Pope's nuncio, informed that the cardinal had
received the viaticum, came to bestow the indulgence "
(p. 264, Paris edition).   This anecdote proves that
gambling, like every other vice, degrades all men to the
same level, and that a negro and a cardinal will both

manifest at death what has been the ruling passion in life. Macpherson, a noted freebooter, who lived during the last century, and was executed at Banff, requested as a last favour to be allowed to play a favourite air, on the scaffold.

When the Dutch abandoned the island in 1712, they left behind them some fugitive slaves, who had escaped to the mountains. These were not left in solitary possession of the island. As soon as it was known that the Dutch had abandoned it, a few husband-men from Bourbon, where a French settlement had been formed in 1657 by M. de Flacourt, after he and his countrymen had been expelled from Madagascar, took possession of it. These, however, were not the sole settlers in Mauritius. Adventurers of all nations, who had been engaged in piracy in the Indian Ocean, and who had formed settlements on the coast of Mada-gascar, flocked to Mauritius, accompanied by their negro wives and slaves. For a period of more than twenty-one years, there was no fixed government. In 1734, the East India Company of France appointed M. de La Bourdonnais, Governor-General, and this truly great man may be regarded as the founder of the colony. It owed its material prosperity and the rapid develop-ment of its resources to his enterprising spirit, his undaunted energy, and his wonderful power of produc-ing the greatest results with the smallest means. He drew up the plan of the present town of Port Louis—he traced roads around the coast and through the in-terior of the island—he organised an army—he instructed the negroes in the art of shipbuilding—and introduced the sugar-cane, the source of the island's future prosperity. He was one of those men, who, if he had lived at an earlier age, and on a more extensive scene, might have been the founder of a dynasty, and had his name handed down to posterity with those of the great heroes of antiquity. Unfortunately for his fame, he lived at a later period, and among Frenchmen. He was recalled, and after being treated with the grossest ingratitude, died of a broken heart. Those who have profited most by his services, have done nothing to express in any permanent form their sense of their value ; but *si monumentum quæris, circumspice.* Mauritius itself is a monument of what may be effected through the talent and energy of one man.

We can only glance at his government in its bearing upon slavery. The East India Company of France, in order to promote agriculture in the colony, had sanctioned the introduction of slaves, whom they sold to the inhabitants at a certain fixed price, This price was seldom paid at the moment of purchase, and, as many evaded payment altogether, La Bourdonnais received instructions on this point, the execution of which made him unpopular among the inhabitants. The slave trade, at this period, was principally in the hands of those pirates who had formed a settlement at Nossé Ibrahim, on the north-east coast of Madagascar, where they had been received with kindness and hospitality by the natives. In return they excited a war between the tribes in the interior and those inhabiting the sea-

coast, and purchased the prisoners made by both for
the purpose of conveying them for sale to Bourbon or
Mauritius. If the prisoners thus obtained proved insufficient to meet the demands of the slave market, a
descent was made on some part of the island, a village
surrounded, and its younger and more vigorous inhabitants borne off to a state of perpetual slavery. Harrowing as the scenes witnessed in such forays must have
been, the slave trade from Madagascar to Mauritius
was not accompanied with the same horrors as from
the neighbouring continent to America. Its victims
were spared the long and harassing march from the
interior, and the horrors of being cooped up for successive weeks beneath the hatches till they reached
their final destination; and yet, of every five negroes
embarked at Madagascar, not more than two were found
fit for service in Mauritius. The rest were either stifled
beneath the hatches, or starved themselves to death, or
died of putrid fever, or became the food of sharks, or
fled to the mountains, or fell beneath the driver's lash.

La Bourdonnais was not the founder of slavery.
The institution preceded his arrival. We have shewn
that the Maroon slaves of the Dutch remained among
the mountains after their masters had left. These
afforded shelter and protection to their countrymen
who escaped from the French. The latter introduced their first slaves in 1723. Slavery thus existed
in Mauritius for more than a century. Of every
eighteen slaves in the colony one died annually, so
that if the traffic had ceased for eighteen years, at

the end of that time the whole black population would have died out. From first to last, Mauritius has been the tomb of more than a million of Africans. Their history is like the roll of the prophet, written within and without, and the writing thereof is mourning, and lamentation, and woe.

In order to check the fugitive slaves, La Bourdonnais employed their countrymen against them, and formed a *maréchaussée*, or mounted police, who protected the colonists from their incursions. To preserve the inhabitants from famine, and render the colony independent of foreign supplies, he introduced the manioc from the island of St Jago and the Brazils, and published an ordinance by which every planter was compelled to cultivate five hundred feet of manioc for every slave that he possessed. The planters, an ignorant and indolent race, used every measure to discredit this innovation, and in some cases destroyed the plantations of manioc by pouring hot water on the root. The benefit conferred by this ordinance was felt and appreciated at an after period, when their crops were destroyed by hurricanes or devoured by locusts. The manioc was safe from either of these casualties, and was the usual article of food for the negroes. La Bourdonnais instructed the slaves in the art of shipbuilding, made them sailors and soldiers, and found them highly useful in the expedition which he undertook against the English in India. He endeavoured, also, to alleviate their sufferings, by the enforcement of the regulations of the Code Noir. After the dispersion of the pirates, the slave trade fell into the hands of European merchants or Creole colonists, who extended it to the adjoining coasts of Africa. The Mozambique negroes were found more tractable than those of Madagascar. The price paid by the French at Madagascar for a man or woman from the age of thirteen to forty, was two muskets, two cartridge-boxes, ten flints, and ten balls, or fifteen hundred balls, or seventeen hundred flints. When the natives became acquainted with the use of money, the usual price was fifty dollars. In 1766, there were about 25,000 slaves and 1200 free coloured persons in the colony. In 1799, there were 55,000 of the former class and 35,000 of the latter. In 1832, they were estimated at 16,000 free coloured persons and 63,536 slaves. It seems difficult to account for the diminution among the free coloured population. Baron Grant states, that to prevent the increase of this class, it was enacted that no slaves should be liberated save those who had saved the lives of their masters. A kind-hearted master could always give his slave an opportunity of saving his life.

The slave trade, barbarous as it was, was not without its incidents of romance. One of these may be briefly related. A young Frenchman, of the name of Grenville had embarked on board a slaver bound for Madagascar, in command of a small detachment of troops. At first they encamped on the small island of Nossé Ibrahim, or St Marie, but were induced by the protestations of a native prince to remove to the mainland. At night Grenville received a visit from the daughter of the prince, who, on the assurance that he would save her life and spare her relations, disclosed to him a plot which her father had formed for the massacre of the whole party. It was to be executed the next day ; the breaking of a stick, which the prince held in his hand, was to be the signal of attack. If he should wish his followers to defer the attack, he would throw his hat towards them. The princess was conducted to a place of safety, and Grenville calmly awaited the result. Everything happened as was foretold. The king made an early visit, carrying in his hand a stick, which after some conversation he broke. To seize him and press a pistol to his head was the work of a moment. His hat was thrown to his attendants, who immediately retired, and he himself was detained in custody till the departure of the vessel. On reaching Mauritius, Grenville, in opposition to his family, publicly married the woman who had saved his life. After some years, intelligence of her father's death reached Mauritius, and she requested permission to visit her native land, which was granted. Her husband, who loved her sincerely, regretted her absence, but refrained from inquiring into the cause. Soon after, the princess returned in the same vessel which had conveyed her to Madagascar, with one hundred and fifty slaves, whom she presented to her husband, with a speech such as might have been expected from one of Corneille's heroines rather than from an uneducated savage. In transferring her subjects to her husband as slaves, she acted the part of a good wife, but of a bad queen.

The first attempt to emancipate the slaves was made by the leaders of the French Revolution, who, while they professed to discard Christianity as a revelation from God, deduced the equality of all men before God from the principles of natural reason. The greatest republic of modern times, which, in its constitution, admits theoretically the equality of all men, and professes to be guided by Christian principles, retains slavery as a domestic institution, and sets public opinion at defiance. Such conduct is a libel on Christianity, and slavery, when defended from revelation, would seem to degrade revelation beneath reason. The founders of the French republic, guided only by reason, struck a blow at slavery as inconsistent with reason: the rulers of the American republic, professing to be guided only by revelation, keep nearly four millions of their fellow-men in bondage, and scout at all interference in their behalf. When shall this foul blot on our modern Christianity be effaced, and Christian Americans enabled to speak and think of their country without a blush?

The prohibition of slavery was rendered null and void by the planters of Mauritius and the members of the local government, all of whom were slaveholders, and opposed to any change. The only effect of the prohibition was to alienate the affection of the colonists from the mother-country, and to lead them to rejoice when Napoleon assumed the consular power, and annulled the ordinance prohibiting slavery. It is a singular coincidence that his nephew, the present French Emperor, has sanctioned the introduction of African immigrants

into the French colonies—a measure which amounts
practically to the repeal of the abolition of slavery, and
will lead to the renewal of the horrors of the slave
trade. It is worthy of remark, that negroes from Madagascar were introduced into Bourbon even before this
traffic was publicly sanctioned by the Imperial Government. Mauritius received one cargo of negroes
recently, when the Government interfered. The planters of both of these colonies have still a hankering after
slavery, and nothing but the keenest watchfulness on
the part of the local authorities can prevent the renewal of this system.

After the capture of the island by the British, the
importation of slaves was prohibited under severe
penalties. As the execution of this law was vested in
the local authorities, who had a direct personal interest
in the continuance of this traffic, slaves were still imported in sufficient numbers to satisfy the wants of
the planters. It is true, that trading in slaves was
declared to be felony—that the two harbours of Port
Louis and Mahébourg were closed against their entrance—that a slave registry was opened in 1815—
and that credulous Governors wrote to the home
authorities that the Mauritians, far from wishing to
renew this nefarious traffic, were filled with indignation
at the remembrance of its horrors. All this may be
true, and yet the slave trade was as brisk as ever, and
the island swarmed with negroes whose peculiar appearance and ignorance of Creole proved them to be of
recent introduction. No law can be executed unless it

be in accordance with the feelings of the community, and the feelings of the Mauritians were altogether in favour of slavery. The illicit introduction of slaves was a felony by law, and yet, notwithstanding the notorious violations of this law, no one was ever convicted. The prisoner might have turned on the judge and proved his complicity in the crime. The only convictions that were obtained were in the case of offenders that were sent to England for trial. This statement will excite no astonishment on the part of those who are acquainted with the manner in which justice is still administered in Mauritius. The slave registry was opened in 1815, but the entries were so falsified, that instead of checking slavery, it threw its mantle of protection over it. Slaves were not introduced publicly at the two chief ports of the island from Africa, but the Seychelles Islands lay at a convenient distance, and slaves registered at the Seychelles were admitted into Mauritius without any questions being asked. The coral reef that surrounds the island could easily be passed, and the slaves landed in those light pirogues that are used by the fishermen. The Governors were surrounded by functionaries who were slaveholders, and who were therefore interested in supporting the traffic, and screening the offenders from punishment; so that their reports, grounded on information received from these parties, were not entitled to much credit. As to the feelings of indignation expressed by the colonists at the remembrance of the horrors of the slave trade, it is sufficient to remark, that rogues are always louder in protestation of their innocence than honest men—that this transition of feeling was too rapid to be sincere—and that truthfulness of character does not stand high in the code of Mauritius morality.

This traffic, ignored or connived at by the local authorities, could not altogether escape the notice of the Home Government; and when the question of compensation to the slaveholders.was under the consideration of the House of Lords, Lord Brougham asked if it were true, that there were 30,000 slaves in Mauritius, the greater part of whom had been imported thither subsequently to the enactment of a law prohibiting the horrid traffic? He wished to know what steps had been taken to ascertain the number of slaves thus illegally imported; whether any measures had been adopted to render it impossible that any one of these slaves should be taken into account in awarding the share of compensation payable to the proprietors under the late act? Lord Glenelg, in reply, admitted that the illegal importation of slaves had been carried on extensively, though he could not say whether the number of slaves thus imported exceeded 30,000. He pointed out the great difficulty which presented itself, in trying to distinguish the slaves illegally imported from others of the same class in the colony. Lord Brougham must say, that if we were to pay £500,000 or £600,000 in respect of illegally imported slaves, or, in other words, for felony and piracy, it would be one of the most hateful operations ever perpetrated in the financial concerns of this country. Hateful as this operation appeared to the noble lord, it was actually perpetrated, and nearly half-a-million of British money was paid in compensation for slaves imported in defiance of British law.   A sum of £2,112,632, 10s. was paid to the slaveholders of Mauritius from the British treasury, as a compensation for the loss sustained through the emancipation of 66,343 slaves.   If the number of slaves illegally imported be estimated at a fourth of the whole number, more than half-a-million of British money was paid to those who, by the law of England, deserved a felon's doom.   It was a masterstroke of Mauritius genius, still looked back to with unqualified admiration, first to introduce some 15,000 slaves in defiance of the laws of Great Britain, and then to make Great Britain pay half-a-million of a compensation for the slaves thus illegally introduced.   But there is a Nemesis in such cases, from whose influence even Mauritians are not exempt.   The large sum thus dishonestly obtained was squandered in luxury and dissipation, and laid the foundation of those extravagant habits among the white Creoles, the indulgence of which, joined with other causes, has led to the transference of a large proportion of the property in the colony from them to their coloured relatives, and may ultimately end in their extinction.

In judging of the treatment of the slaves in Mauritius, recourse·must be had to those writers who visited or lived in the colony during the prevalence of slavery, and have given the world the benefit of their experience.   These are St Pierre, Sonnerat, and Baron

Grant. The first of these, the well-known author of " Paul and Virginia," whose works contributed largely to the abolition of slavery by the founders of the first republic, spent several years in the island, and mingled freely with the inhabitants of all classes. The last was born in the colony, where his father had sought to retrieve his fortune after the failure of Law's Mississippi scheme. As the son of a slaveholder, who had been accustomed from infancy to witness the cruelties to which the negroes were exposed, Grant endeavours in every way to soften the picture, or to justify the darker shades which cannot be concealed, on the ground of necessity. St Pierre, on the other hand, was an enthusiastic young man, with a heart overflowing with those sentiments of humanity which, in theory at least, pervaded all classes of society in France towards the commencement of the eighteenth century. An enthusiastic admirer of Nature, which nowhere presents herself to the eye of the traveller under more fascinating forms than in Mauritius, he could not help contrasting her peaceful aspect with the fearful cruelties which he daily witnessed, and feeling that while all God's other works were perfect in their beauty, man alone was vile. While slavery sheds its baleful influences over all countries where it has ever existed, and leaves unmistakeable traces of its presence and character, it is a strange fact, which we leave to others to explain, that the French, who are, in theory, the most humane of all nations, have, in practice, been the most cruel in the treatment of their slaves, with the exception perhaps of the Spaniards, who seem to vie with them for this evil notoriety. The pictures presented in the writings of St Pierre might appear exaggerated, or prejudiced, if drawn by a foreigner; but it must be borne in mind, that he describes only what he witnessed, and that his good faith has never been questioned. He thus speaks of their landing and treatment:—"They are landed with just a rag round their loins. The men are ranged on one side and the women on the other, with their infants, who cling from fear to their mothers. The planter, having examined them as he would a horse, buys what may then attract him. Brothers, sisters, friends, lovers, are now torn asunder, and bidding each other a long farewell, are driven weeping to the plantations they are bought for. Sometimes they turned desperate, fancying that the white people intended eating their flesh, making red wine of their blood, and powder of their bones. They were treated in the following manner:—At break of day a signal of three smacks of a whip called them to work, when each betook himself with his spade to the plantation, where they worked almost naked in the heat of the sun. Their food was bruised or boiled maize, or bread made of manioc, a root for which we have no name in Europe; their clothing a single piece of linen. Upon the commission of the most trivial offence, they were tied hands and feet to a ladder, where the overseer approached with a whip like a postilion's, and gave them fifty, a hundred, or perhaps two hundred lashes upon the back. Each stroke carried off its portion of skin. The poor wretch was then untied, an iron collar with three spikes put round his neck, and he was then sent back to his task. Some of them were unable to sit down for a month after this beating —a punishment inflicted with equal severity on women as on men. In the evening, when they returned home, they were obliged to pray for the prosperity of their masters, and wish them a good night before they retired to rest. (There is a refinement of cruelty in these forced prayers worse than the lash itself.) There was a law in force in their favour called the Code Noir, which ordained that they should receive no more than thirty lashes for any one offence—that they should not work on Sundays—that they should eat meat once a-week, and have a new shirt every year; but this was not observed."

In America, and other countries distant from the continent where slaves are produced, self-interest leads the slaveholder to feed his slaves with sufficient food, that, like well-fed beasts of burden, they may do their work well. In Mauritius there was no such motive; the slave-producing country was within a few days' sailing, and the supply inexhaustible. As slaves were abundant and provisions dear, the great problem was to extract from them the maximum of labour, and to feed them at the minimum of expense. On this point M. Sonnerat remarks—" I have known humane and compassionate masters who, instead of maltreating them, tried to mitigate their servile condition, but they are very few in number.

The rest exercise over their negroes a cruel and revolting tyranny. The slave, after having laboured the whole day, sees himself obliged to search for his food in the woods, and lives only on unwholesome roots. They die of misery and bad treatment, without exciting the smallest feeling of pity, and consequently they never let slip any opportunity of breaking their chains in order to escape to the forests in search of independence and misery." So miserable was their existence that they welcomed death as a friend, and often committed crime in the hope of being executed. Montgomery Martin mentions the case of one who broke his master's furniture in his absence, in the hope that, on his returning home, he would run him through with his sword. St Pierre saw a woman throw herself from the top of a ladder, and others, broken alive, endure that horrible punishment without a cry. A better idea of their treatment may be derived from the "Code Noir," which was drawn up for their protection, than from citing isolated cases of cruelty. This Code Noir was well named: intended to repress cruelty, it is itself one of the darkest records of human cruelty. On perusing its different articles, the thought naturally suggests itself, What must have been the cruelties of slavery, when this Code, every page of which seems written in blood, was drawn up from feelings of humanity?

"Art. 27. The slave who strikes his master, his mistress, or their children, with contusion or effusion of blood, or in the face, shall be punished with death.

" Art. 28. And as to attacks or assaults committed by slaves against free persons, it is our will that they be severely punished, even with death, if such a case occurs.

" Art. 32. The fugitive slave absent for a month, counting from the day when his master has denounced him to justice, shall have his ears cut, and be marked with a *fleur de lys* on one of his shoulders; and if he commit the same offence during another month, counting in the same way from the day of denunciation, he shall be hamstrung, and marked with a *fleur de lys* on his other shoulder; and the third time, he shall be punished with death.

" Art. 38. All our subjects of the said countries, of whatever quality and condition they may be, are hereby prohibited from torturing their slaves by their own private authority, or from causing them to be tortured under any pretext whatever, or from mutilating any of their members, or causing them to be mutilated, under the penalty of having the slaves confiscated, and being proceeded against by special process; be it lawful for them only, when they believe that their slaves have merited it, to put them in chains, and to beat them with rods or ropes." If these laws were considered humane, what must have been the enormities of the system which they were meant to repress!

The love of music and dancing is so deeply rooted in the heart of the African, that even slavery could not extinguish it. It might have been expected that the slaveholder, satisfied with the labours of his slaves during the day, would have left them some hours of relaxation during the night. "Sometimes they appointed a rendezvous in the middle of the night, and, under the shelter of a rock, danced to the dismal sound of a bladder filled with peas; but the approach of a white person, or the bark of a dog, immediately broke up the assembly. They had also dogs with them, and these animals knew perfectly, even in the dark, not only the white man, but the dog that belonged to him, both of whom they feared and hated, and howled as soon as they appeared. The dogs of the whites seemed on their parts to have adopted the sentiments of their masters, and at the least encouragement, would fly with the utmost fury upon a slave or his dog."* The Code Noir had its punishment for these assemblies:—" Slaves belonging to different masters are prohibited from assembling by day or by night, under pain of corporal punishment, which cannot be less than whipping or the *fleur de lys;* and in case of frequent repetitions of the offence, and other aggravating circumstances, they may be punished with death: this is left to the will of the judges." Thus the law gave the slaveholder the power of control over his slave by day and by night, and made him his " chattel" as much as the spade with which he dug the earth. Many of these poor creatures were roused to such a state of despair, that all ordinary means failed to give expression to their anguished feelings. On the quay St Pierre saw some of them so overpowered with grief,

* St Pierre.

that no burning tear or suffering cry could give them relief, and in silent despair they bit the cannon to which they were tied, like mad dogs.

It might have been expected that the softer sex, whose hearts are ever ready to overflow with sympathy at the sight of human suffering, would have done much to alleviate the miserable condition of the slave. It is with sincere regret that we are compelled to state, that the records of slavery present woman less in the guise of a guardian angel, watching over the poor slave, and speaking words of womanly sympathy and hope, than in that of an avenging fury, brandishing the whip and causing it to drink the black man's blood. There could not be a stronger argument against the system of slavery than its power to transform one whom God has endowed with a softer and finer organisation than man, with a readier sympathy and a warmer heart, into a being who resembles more the dark creations of heathen mythology than the sober realities of actual life. Female slaveholders shewed a power of invention and a refinement of cruelty in the punishment of their slaves to which the stronger but less imaginative sex failed to attain. The estate is still pointed out in the district of Flacq, on which an act of cruelty was perpetrated which has no counterpart in the annals of crime. A young negress had excited the jealousy of her mistress, through the attentions which she received from her husband. In the absence of the latter, his wife caused the slave to be seized and baked to death in an oven. A Creole lady, dressed as an Amazon, used to join the parties that went in search of the fugitive slaves, and to shoot them down wherever she found them. St Pierre alludes to the case of a female slave, who ran up to him one day, and throwing herself at his feet, besought his intercession with her mistress. She was obliged to sit up so late at night, and to rise so early in the morning, that she could find no time for sleep ; and if she happened to allow herself to drop asleep during the day, her mistress caused her lips to be rubbed with ordure. If she failed to lick this off she was consigned to the lash. At St Pierre's intercession she was promised more lenient treatment; but after his departure was probably treated with still greater severity, as the utterance of a complaint was considered a crime, and punished as such. On another occasion he had paid a visit to a Creole lady, when, her dogs happening to quarrel, she commanded a slave to separate them. As he did not shew sufficient alacrity in obeying her orders, she seized a branch of a prickly shrub, with which she struck the dog and the slave with such effect, that the one ran howling away and the other was covered with blood. "It seemed to be a pretty general opinion that the cruelest of owners were old women, and those who had been slaves themselves. One instance of the former was notorious at Mahébourg. In the immediate neighbourhood of that village there resided a Madame de ——, I forget her name—a rich, avaricious, high-born, cruel old lady. She had a fine estate, beautifully situated on high

grounds, overlooking the bay; it was in the highest
state of cultivation, and she owned some hundreds of
slaves, who, meet them where you might, could be at
once distinguished by the prominence of their ribs and
vertebræ, the haggard melancholy of their looks, and
not unfrequently by the wheals on their backs. The
whole country rang with stories of her cruelties, perpetrated in secret floggings, in which the old fiend
gloated over the agonies of her victims, and sometimes condescended, it was said, to operate herself."—
Voyage to Mauritius.

The amount of crime committed by the slaves is
small, if the treatment to which they were subjected
is taken into account. They were accused of being
such gluttons that they stole victuals from the neighbouring houses; but this charge proves only the
sordid character of their masters, who did not provide them with sufficient food. When too old to
labour they were turned out of doors, to find their food
as best they might. St Pierre saw a miserable old
creature, all skin and bone, cutting off the flesh of a
dead horse to eat. They were accused of being so idle
that they took no manner of interest in their master's
business, and rarely performed what they were set
about. It must be remembered, however, that their
labour was compulsory, that they had no personal interest in the matter, and received no reward for their
services. A French slaveholder, transported to Madagascar, and obliged to labour as a slave beneath a broil-
ing sun, would probably have been as idle and disobe-

dient. Their women were accused of preferring to destroy
their children rather than bring them into the world.
This charge, if true, proves how horrible must have
been the working of a system that could overpower the
maternal instinct, and make the poor mother prefer
death to her offspring, to training them up as a race of
slaves. They were guilty at times of arson and poison-
ing, the latter a crime difficult of detection, from their
acquaintance with the many poisonous plants, common
to Mauritius and Madagascar. But then there is a
point beyond which the human mind, if unsustained
by Christian principle, can endure no longer, and seeks
relief either in the annihilation of self or the removal
of the cause of suffering. But the most common
offence with which the slaves are charged, is that of
marronage, or escaping from their masters. And why
should they not? The love of liberty is one of the
most powerful passions implanted in the human heart,
and there was no principle of affection or gratitude to
bind them to their masters. Certain death, after a few
years of liberty and misery among the mountains, was
the best fate that they could expect. They were hunted
down like wild beasts, and shot without mercy. The lives
and property of their former masters were in a measure
in their power, and yet the crimes of arson and murder
were rare, when compared to the temptation. Sometimes when these Maroons were attacked, the women
saved the lives of the men by the sacrifice of their own
liberty. St Pierre saw two negro women at the house
of a planter, who had saved the life of a fugitive slave,

by throwing themselves with tears at the planter's feet, and thus affording their companion an opportunity of escape, at the moment when he was about to be put to death.

Another mode of desertion was to seize upon a pirogue or fishing boat, and to make for Madagascar, which is about five hundred miles distant from Mauritius. "They seemed," says Grant, "to have had an instinctive knowledge that the distance of the country was not in proportion to the length of the voyage, and would direct their hands to the point where it lay, and exclaim in their corrupted French, " Ça blanc là li beaucoup malin; li couri beaucoup dans la mer là haut, mais Magascar li là."* This opinion sometimes incited them to undertake the most desperate actions, and they would make the most daring attempts to return to their homes. Sometimes they would regard us with a most ferocious aspect, as they have adopted the belief, since the affair at Port Dauphin, in their island, that the wine we drink is the blood of negroes. After their escape into the mountains and forests of the Isle of France, they would endeavour to get possession of a canoe or other small boat, along the coast, wherever they could find it, and shewed not only uncommon courage, but also address and activity, in putting to sea. At other times they contrived to make a large pirogue or canoe of a single tree, some of which are large in this island, and in one of these they would trust to the mercy

* "The white man is very cunning; he runs about a great deal in that direction, but Madagascar is there."

of the waves, and attempt a passage to Madagascar, nearly five hundred miles distant, with a mere calabash of water and a few manioc or cassada roots. It has also happened that when they have found themselves too numerous for the canoe to contain them with safety, they would alternately embark and swim through the voyage." Though many of these adventurers were lost, some of them have been known, by the force of the currents and the favour of the winds, which generally blew that way, to have regained their native land, having been recognised by French people who had seen them at Mauritius. Sometimes they have even been known to make for the continent itself, over the stormy and pathless ocean; and though the majority perished, some succeeded. Such were the extremities these ill-fated beings resorted to, to escape from an existence absolutely insupportable.*

Similar attempts seem to have been made at a later period to escape from the Seychelles Islands, where the slaves were treated with the same harshness as in Mauritius. Montgomery Martin relates that H.M.S. *Barracouta* picked up a frail canoe made out of a single tree, near the equator, and another about a hundred miles off the coast of Africa; it contained five runaway slaves, one dying in the bottom of the canoe, and the other four nearly exhausted. They had fled from a harsh French master at the Seychelles, committed themselves to the deep without compass or guide, with a small quantity of

* Pridham, St Pierre, &c.

water and rice, and trusting to their fishing-lines for support. Steering by the stars, they had nearly reached the coast from which they had been kidnapped, when nature sunk exhausted; and the *Barracouta* just arrived in time to save four of their lives. So long as the wanderers in search of home were able to do so, the days were numbered by notches on the side of the canoe, and twenty-one were thus marked, when met with by the British vessel.

It could scarcely be expected that Christianity should have made much progress among the slaves, seeing that they met with such treatment at the hands of men professedly Christian, or that the prayers which they were compelled to offer up every evening for the welfare of their masters could have been uttered with much sincerity. Apart from this form, in itself a mere mockery, they seem to have known little or nothing of Christianity. They retained the superstitions and practised the idolatrous rites peculiar to their native land. Like the Chinese, they had a peculiar and extravagant feeling of respect for their ancestors, and it was an unpardonable insult to speak disrespectfully of their kindred. They were in the habit of casting lots for the purpose of gaining an insight into the events of the future. They usually bore about their persons some object—it might be a small piece of wood or of cloth—which was regarded as a talisman or charm, and known by the name of *grisgris*. Many, at the present day, of those who are nominally Christians, wear these *grisgris*, which they use much in the same way as the Roman

Catholics do their rosaries. The marriage ceremony was occasionally performed, the planter being the officiating priest. It consisted simply in a recommendation of mutual fidelity and forbearance, with a threat of the lash should either party violate its engagements. Of course the recommendation of the planter would have much effect, being in such excellent keeping with his own example and daily life. Any neglect of this recommendation in the case of the males was punished with the driver's whip; in the case of the females the whip was handed to the husband, who had usually the magnanimity to forgive his wife.

Their only period of rejoicing was at the commencement of a new year. This festival, still known and observed under the name of "Le Banani," resembled in some respects the saturnalia of the Romans. It derived its name, not from the French word for a year, but from the fruit of the bananier, or banana tree, of which the slaves were very fond, and with which they were permitted to gorge themselves on this festive occasion. So pleasant were their reminiscences of this indulgence, that they were in the habit of reckoning time, not by years, but by the number of banana feasts which they had enjoyed. This festival is still observed, and negro servants, who are tolerably sober during the rest of the year, claim the right of getting drunk for three days on this occasion, which is a period of general license, shared in by the Coolie immigrants as well as the descendants of the slaves.

Attachment to their native land was not a mere sentiment; it was incorporated with, and formed part of, their religious belief. They believed that when the soul quitted the body it returned not to God, but to the place of their birth, there to exist under some other form—a belief, perhaps, traditionally connected with the doctrine of the metempsychosis which has exercised such a powerful influence over the inhabitants of the East. The desire that their bodies should be interred in their native land was perhaps as influential as the love of liberty in inducing many of them to put to sea, and thus expose themselves to a lingering death. This desire, probably connected in some way with their religious belief, is still prevalent among the inhabitants of Madagascar. When Radama led an army of 50,000 men into the lowlands of Madagascar, every five soldiers bound themselves by a solemn vow, that the survivors should carry back the bones of those who died or were slain, so as that their ashes might mingle with those of their forefathers. The pestilential fevers engendered by the swampy plains that surround the sea-coast, cut off nearly 40,000 of his followers, and the survivors, regarding their promise as sacred, bore back their flesh-less bones to their native place.

They seem to have regarded the monkeys, with which Mauritius abounds, as a species of the human race, possessed of superior abilities to themselves, but cautiously concealing their talents for fear that the planters might reduce them to slavery. It was a common remark among them—"Ah! Zacko beaucoup malin, li n'a pas voulé causer, li conné bien, si li causer, li blanc li faîre travailler;"—"Jacko is very cunning, he won't speak; he knows very well that if he spoke the white man would make him work." The language spoken by the slaves was a species of broken French, intermingled with words belonging to the different dialects spoken in their native land. It differed considerably from modern Creole, which has been enriched by the contributions which it has levied from English, Hindustanee, and the different languages of the Indian peninsula, so as to become a complicated lingual *olla podrida*, the analysis and dissection of the component parts of which will puzzle the philologist of future ages. The crushing influences of slavery could not repress the negro's innate love of music and song, which found vent in a species of poetry remarkable for its quaint simplicity. A gentleman belonging to the colony, M. Crétien, made a collection of these negro songs, which are worthy of the examination of all who are interested in the construction of languages by a primitive and half-savage race. The following song, celebrating the few joys of which slavery admitted, will give an idea of the Creole spoken by the negroes:—

I.

" Moi resté dans en p'tit la caze
 Qu'il faut baissé moi pour entré
 Mon la tête touché son faitaze
 Quand mon le pié touché plancé
 Moi té n'a pas besoin lumière
 Le soir quand moi voulé dormi,
 Car pour moi trouvé lune claire,
 N'a pas manqué trous Dié merci.

II.

" Mon lit est un p'tit natt' Malgace
Mon l'oriellé morceau bois blanc,
Mon gargoulette un'vié cabbase,
Ou moi met l'arack, zour de l'an,
Quand mon femm' pour fair' p'tit ménaze,
Sam' di, comme ça vini soupé
Moi fair' cuir dans mon p'tit la caze
Banane sous la cendr' grillé.

III.

" A mon coffre n'a pas serrure
Et jamais moi n'a fermé li.
Dans bambou comme ça sans ferrure
Qui'va cherché mon langousi?
Mais dimanche si gagné zournée
Moi l'achette morceau d'tabac
Et tout la s'maine moi fais fumée
Dans grand pipe, a moi carouba."

This unique production would suffer by translation.

The condition of the slave population was gradually
improved till the year 1829, when an ordinance of the
Governor in Council conferred most important benefits
upon them, and paved the way for their emancipation.
When that period arrived, great anxiety was felt by the
planters lest there should be some outbreak, or attempt
to retaliate for the injuries which they had endured.
The event proved that there was no ground for such
apprehensions.   The negro is naturally a forgiving
animal, and his joy at finding himself at length a free
man, and being permitted to wear shoes as a symbol
of liberty, absorbed every other feeling.   Those who
obtained their freedom, assumed rather patronising
airs towards those still in a state of slavery.   An amusing instance of this is related by Mr Backhouse, but to

appreciate it thoroughly, one must have witnessed the mock-airs of dignity which negroes assume towards those whom they esteem to be their inferiors.   An emancipated slave was familiarly addressed by one of his former comrades, still a slave, "Do you not see that I am a white man?" was the haughty rejoinder.   "Look in the fountain, and behold your face."   "Ah, but look at my feet, and behold my shoes."   Leather, not colour, was the test of freedom.   Instead of the emancipated slaves committing outrages on their former masters, the reverse of this seems to have sometimes occurred. Backhouse alludes to the case of a negress, who had been shot at and wounded by order of her former master, as she was leaving his premises, because she had bought up the residue of her term of apprenticeship.   No punishment was inflicted on her cowardly assailant. The man who had taken her into his house acknow- ledged that his conscience was uneasy at having con- cealed some outrages against slaves, that had come to his knowledge, but, when called upon to give evidence in this case, he declined.   The chief charge against the negroes, after their emancipation, was that their women, instead of working in the fields as they had been wont to do before, preferred remaining at home and nursing their children.   This appeared singular to Mauritius planters, who regarded them as destitute of maternal affection, but English mothers will judge leniently of their conduct in this respect.

More than twenty years have now elapsed since the abolition of slavery, and the evil passions evoked by that act of tardy justice have already in a great measure subsided, if not died out in Mauritius. Whatever effect that measure may have produced in other British colonies, in Mauritius it cannot be regarded as otherwise than a positive blessing both to the slave and to the planter. It gave to the one liberty, and to the other wealth. It is a singular fact, that during the existence of slavery, with the slave market almost at their doors, and every facility for the importation of negroes, the planters of Mauritius were and continued to be poor, while, after the emancipation, through the introduction of free labourers from India, those of them who have not become the victims of luxury or usury, have attained a degree of material prosperity previously unknown. In a word the more enlightened among them admit that free labour is cheaper and more economical than slave labour, and that the immense quantity of sugar now annually exported could never have been produced under the system of slavery. Every year witnesses fresh inroads upon the forests, and the formation of new plantations, the capital expended on which may always be recovered by good management in the course of a few years. The Abbé Raynal states, that this colony, while in the possession of the French, instead of paying its own expenses, cost France eight millions of livres annually, and recommends that this settlement, as well as Bourbon, should be abandoned. In 1855, the revenue of the colony was £348,452, and its expenditure £317,839, leaving a surplus of £30,613. The accumulation of surplus revenue in the treasury from 1850 to 1855, amounted to £161,915. If the planters have not all as satisfactory a balance in their favour at their bankers, it is because some of them, of late years, have indulged in a reckless expenditure, which could not fail to involve them in difficulties. If the effect of the abolition of slavery had been exactly the opposite—if instead of raising the colony from comparative poverty to a degree of unprecedented prosperity, it had plunged it into inextricable difficulties—the justice of that measure would have been still the same. That measure was not grounded on expediency, but on a principle often acted on before, but first enunciated by Lord Mansfield. *Fiat justitia, ruat cœlum.*

That their emancipation was an unqualified blessing to the negroes, no one, who compares their past with their present condition, can for a moment doubt. The most of the old race of ex-apprentices have died out, and those who remain in many cases bear on their bodies proofs of the workings of slavery more convincing than the pages even of St Pierre. When they found themselves their own masters, the former slaves preferred supporting themselves by cultivating small patches of land in the highlands of Moka and Vacoua, to labouring in the fields of their former masters. If they had acted otherwise, they would have shewn themselves unworthy of liberty; it would have been like a galley slave resuming the oar, when told that he was free. Their descendants have been much blamed for manifesting the same antipathy against agricultural labour, but without reason. "You ask me," said a negro, whose father and mother had been slaves, "why I will not work in that field—I will tell you: In that field my father worked as a slave, and was lashed as a slave, and do you think that I would work upon a spot that I cannot think of without pain?" If a planter had had the misfortune to be hanged, his son would scarcely select as the site for a new house the place where the scaffold was erected. We should be just to the negro, and remember that he is a man with the same feelings as other men.

The descendants of the slaves have become the mechanics, the shopkeepers, the fishermen, the coachmen, and the market gardeners of the colony. In these different capacities, they obtain far higher wages than are paid to the Coolie immigrants, who are employed as agricultural labourers. The lowest class of labourers, who are employed in unloading the ships, can make a dollar a-day with rations; and it is scarcely to be expected that they should work in the fields at a lower rate of wages. They are not so industrious or enterprising as the same class in Europe, but their wants are so few and simple, that they can be easily supplied by two days' labour every week. Few people labour with their hands from the mere love of labour, and if the poor negro can make enough to supply his daily wants, he is philosopher enough to be satisfied. He only labours that he may enjoy with the produce of his labour that *dolce far' niénte*, which he esteems the highest happiness of which his nature is capable.

This class have adopted all the exaggerated forms of politeness practised by the white Creoles; and really the principle of imitation is so admirably developed in the negro, that they go through all the different modes of salutation with a stately gravity which leaves little to desire. It is amusing to see two old slaves, who are friends, meet one another in the street. The soldier's battered shako worn as Paddy wore his coat, or the old hat coeval, perhaps, with La Bourdonnais, is gracefully raised from the head, and, after mutual *salaams* and shakings of the hand, affectionate inquiries are made about *Madame*, and the other members of their respective families. Sometimes, from no apparent cause, except perhaps an exuberance of animal spirits and a thorough enjoyment of their present liberty, or appreciation of their own highly polished manners, they burst forth into fits of inextinguishable laughter. Their laughter is irresistible. It is like the uncorking of a champagne bottle or the gushing forth of waters from a fountain. It rises from the depths of the African's interior, expands his chest, swells his throat, lights up his eye, opens his mouth, exhibits his teeth, and then after certain convulsive throes, comes bubbling forth like sparkling wine from a narrow-necked bottle. It is not like ordinary cachinnation, the affair of a moment, performed without cessation from the work in hand. His laughter is so to speak a serious affair, which unfits him for every kind of labour and absorbs all his faculties. He looks as if some chemical process was going on within him, resulting in the production of laughing gas, and causing involuntary explosions. His whole body shakes under the influence of the laughing demon that has seized upon him; and it is sometimes a quarter of an hour before the fit is over. You may see no cause for laughter. You may have addressed him in the gravest manner without thinking of laughing yourself, or of being the cause of laughter in others. And yet some invisible agency has affected his risible faculties, and off he goes, hick! hick! till sometimes he rolls upon the ground in an agony of convulsive enjoyment. Like Charles Lamb, when he elicited the laughter of the young sweep by his fall, you feel rather pleased at being the involuntary cause of so much mirth to such a miserable creature. You may be hungry or pressed for time, yet his laugh is irresistible. It is so thoroughly infectious, that you must join in it through pure sympathy. We believe that Heraclitus himself could not have resisted a negro's laugh; and that if Uncle Tom had known how to give a hearty *guffaw* at the right time, even Legree could not have found it in his heart to whip him to death.

The *ci-devant* slave population and their descendants retain their original taste for dancing and music. Evening reunions for dancing, though not so frequent as immediately after the emancipation of the slaves, are still highly popular. These assemblages are objectionable in many respects, and the Roman Catholic priests have very properly set their faces against them. No race has naturally a finer ear or a keener enjoyment of the

charms of music than the African.   The military band
plays on the Champ de Mars once a-week, and there
is always a large circle of blacks listening to the music.
It is evidently thoroughly appreciated and enjoyed,
especially by those *gamins* that seem as indigenous to
the streets of Port Louis as to those of Paris.   Their
merry black eyes sparkle with pleasure, their heads and
feet move in harmony with the music, and sometimes
they describe somersets in a kind of ecstasy of enjoyment.   The quickness and correctness of the African
ear would be almost incredible to those who have not
observed the rapidity with which they master the
intricacies of the most difficult pieces of music.   When
a new piece of music has caught the popular ear, it is
no unusual thing to hear it whistled from beginning to
end with perfect accuracy by boys who have only heard
it once or twice.   I have heard the opera of " Lucia di
Lammermoor" performed in this way by a band of
workmen engaged in their labours.   Each one had his
part, waited his turn, and struck in with a precision and
correctness that might have done honour to a well-
trained orchestra.   When this primitive music was
performed by tailors, it was amusing to observe the
stitching increasing or diminishing in rapidity with
the time observed in the opera, and the perfect gravity
with which these blackbirds "warbled forth their wood-
notes wild."   Their masters encourage them in their
musical propensities, finding that the slowness of the
work when the music is slow is compensated for by
its rapidity when the music is quick, and that when

there is no music, there is more chattering and laughing than work. Many of them are no mean performers on the violin and violoncello. The instruments used by their fathers were of a simple character. Besides the bladder filled with peas alluded to by St Pierre, I have seen three kinds of musical instruments used by the ex-apprentices, and common enough formerly, though now rather rare. The first consists of a number of reeds of the same length, skilfully joined together, and resembling in shape "Pan's pipes," though on a much larger scale. The performer holds the instrument by the end, and discourses a species of music, the beauty of which is perceptible only to the initiated. I have only seen it played once; the performer was an old ex-apprentice, probably the last minstrel of his race. The second resembles a small violin, with this difference that it has only one string. One evening, in walking up the valley of the Pouce, my attention was attracted by a species of suppressed humming, like the noise made by a bumbee. On approaching the place from which the sound proceeded, I found an old grizzly-headed negro strumming on his one string, and singing a Creole song. I respectfully requested this modern Paganini to exhibit the powers of his instrument, which, after some excuses, prompted no doubt by that modesty which distinguishes all great performers, he did. On observing my suppressed laughter, he slunk away, thinking, perhaps, with other unappreciated geniuses, thet he lived in an age which was unworthy of him. The third was a sort of rudely-constructed guitar, played

by a native of Madagascar, while he sung one of the
songs of the Hovas.

The three besetting sins of every slave population
are lying, drunkenness, and dishonesty.   The *ci-devant*
slaves and their descendants have not yet been able to
cast them aside.   A strict adherence to truth is not
a leading feature in the character of any portion of
the Creole population of Mauritius, and the blacks are
just what the system of slavery made them.   They
have never been taught to speak the truth, and when
they do speak it, it is only when they stumble on it by
accident.   The Roman Catholic bishop, whose position
entitles his opinion on this subject to much weight, in
a return made to the Legislature, scrupled to name
more than two who could be received as evidence upon
oath.   If some modern Diogenes were to start with his
lanthorn, he would find it very difficult to discover these
two men.   Either of them would be a *rara avis in
terris*, and very like a black swan.

The want of money prevented the slaves from indulging largely in drunkenness, except at the great
annual festival.   Their large earnings and the numerous
canteens situated at the corners of almost every street,
place temptations in their way from which they were
formerly exempt.   And yet they must be regarded, on
the whole, as a far more sober and temperate class than
the working-men of our cities at home.   I have never
seen any of them drunk on the streets except the lowest
class of blacks employed about the bazaar and the
shipping, and their conduct in this respect forms a

favourable contrast to that of the British soldiers and sailors, who may be seen staggering in the streets at any hour of the day.

On examining the statistics of crime since the abolition of slavery, one cannot avoid being struck with its apparent increase. A closer analysis, however, will shew that almost all the heavier charges have been brought against Indians, of whom nearly a hundred thousand have been introduced into the colony within the last twenty years. In the course of six years, I knew of only one case of murder committed by a negro, who was executed, and another of culpable homicide. Pilfering, or petty theft, is the most common offence charged against the negroes. Acting on M. Prudhomme's principle, *La propriété c'est le vol*, they endeavour to indemnify themselves for the injuries they have received at the hands of society by appropriating all the poultry, fruit, and vegetables they can lay their hands upon. The Roman Catholic priests have failed to teach them a sounder morality, though they have introduced the confessional as a sort of mental torture to deter them from dishonesty. Many ludicrous instances are cited of the manner in which the searching examination of the confessional is sometimes eluded by negro cunning. The following may serve as an example, though its force is much weakened by translation:—A priest in the country had had his poultry-yard cleared at different times of all its feathery tenants, from the speckled guinea-fowl to the tender turkey which he had reserved for his own Christmas dinner. Suspecting that the

thieves were among his own flock, he assembled his
brebis noirs for confession.   The first penitent was the
man who had stolen the turkey, with which he had
feasted his friends there assembled.   After some time
he came forth, perspiring at every pore, and panting
with excitement.   The contest had been a keen one,
and he had to relate his experience to the others, who
had to pass through the same fiery ordeal.   " Him say,
' Do you ever steal ducks ?'   Me say, ' Never, father ;
me never steal ducks.'   ' Do you ever steal geese ?'
' Never, father ; me never steal geese.'   ' Do you ever
steal guinea-fowls or chickens ?'   ' Never, father ; me
never steal guinea-fowl or chicken.'   ' Good; me
absolve you.   Go.'   But (here there was a shout of
laughter, heartily shared in by his audience), the
good father! he never ask if me stole turkeys ; "—
("Mais li bon père! li n'a pas demandé, si moi fin
volé di' dindes").

CHAPTER III.

THE coloured population, under which designation are
included all those who have a mixture of European and
African blood in their veins, form a very important
part of the Mauritius community.   Their existence
dates from the origin of the colony.   The pirates from
Madagascar brought with them their negro wives and
coloured offspring, and the adventurers who flocked to
it from Europe were rarely restrained by moral or religious principles from the indulgence of their passions.
They introduced female slaves from the coast of Africa
and the neighbouring island of Madagascar, who occupied the ambiguous position of being at once the mis-
tresses and the slaves of their purchasers.   The children
were the slaves of their fathers, and could be sold as
other slaves; but paternal affection often led the parents

to effect their liberty, and at death to bequeath to them their property. Hence arose a third class, distinct from the European and African races, but having the blood of both circulating in their veins, and partaking largely of the character of both. The face is the face of Japhet, but the skin is the skin of Ham, varying in colour from the darkest ebony, where the regular features mark a mixture of European blood, to the purest white, where tradition alone preserves the remembrance of the presence of African blood. The antipathy against the smallest admixture of African blood amounts to a positive passion. A man may have wealth, learning, official rank, all that elsewhere can command respect, and yet let there be but three drops of African blood in his veins, tradition will preserve the remembrance of them, and point to these as the plague-spot, the touch of which would be pollution. Marriage with such a man would be a voluntary act of Pariahism on the part of a white woman, and lead to her exclusion from the society of all the *purs sangs* in the colony. In Europe, we often hear of noble blood ; but in Mauritius, all blood that circulates in white men's veins is noble, and the taint of colour the only bar sinister. Between the white and coloured population there exists a feeling of bitter hatred, the result of long years of domination and insult on the one hand, and subjection and suffering on the other. Under the French Government, the coloured people were subjected to many humiliations, which were keenly felt by a class naturally vain and ambitious of social equality. The white man might insult the coloured man with impunity; the code of honour justified the former in refusing to accept a challenge from the latter, if he had the presumption to have recourse to such a means of redress. If a coloured man met a white man in the street, he was obliged to leave the pavement and salute him by lifting his hat. In the militia, formed for the defence of the island, no man of colour could bear arms in a company of white men, and he was prohibited from sending his children to the college attended by the children of the other class. Death is generally supposed to overturn all social distinctions, and to place all men on the same level; but the antipathy to colour extended even beyond death, and prevented the ashes of the coloured man from reposing beside those of his white brother. While these invidious distinctions have now been in a great measure obliterated, the feelings of hostility between the two classes are still as inveterate and deeply rooted as before. Apart from the antipathy to colour which every white man feels, and which every good man will subdue, other causes have led to this estrangement between two classes that have so much in common. The antipathy to colour felt by the white Creole women is stronger than that exhibited by the other sex, and has led them to refuse to associate with the coloured population in any way. One cannot avoid sympathising, to a certain extent, with the feeling that has led them to adopt this measure of exclusion. The respectable Sarahs of Mauritius married life could scarcely regard with a favourable eye the dusky Hagars and sepia-coloured Ishmaels with whom their husbands' licentiousness surrounded them. After the island came into the possession of the British, and the galling social distinctions before alluded to were overturned, the coloured women endeavoured to indemnify themselves for previous insults by outstripping the white in the luxury of their toilettes and the splendour of their equipages. They took possession of the fashionable drive on the Champ de Mars, and the first seats in the theatre. The white women, scorning to enter into open rivalry with a race that they despised, withdrew from all the places which they frequented, and induced their husbands (who, having relations with both parties, were disposed to remain neutral) to take up the quarrel. Jealous of seeing their wives outshone by a class whom they esteemed to be little better than slaves, the husbands refused to recognise the coloured women in public, or to admit them to their houses. Passion, however, was more powerful than prejudice, and the secret *liaisons* between the white men and the coloured women were continued. Those who were unmarried bequeathed their property to their coloured offspring, and thus strengthened the feeling of ill-will which their relatives already entertained against the coloured people. It has been already shewn how, in this way, about three-fourths of the immoveable property in the colony has been transferred from the white to the coloured population, and this transference has naturally widened the gulf between them. They have also come into collision in the arena of political strife. The white French population are, from language, habit, and association, passionately attached to the land which gave their fathers birth. The Governor of Bourbon, after a recent visit, truthfully described the island as *boiling with French feeling*, and his intercourse was confined to the white population, who make no concealment of their desire to see the Union Jack replaced by the Tricolor. The coloured population, on the other hand, who owe their enjoyment of equal rights, and their immunity from previous wrongs, to the British Government, are loud in their professions of loyalty and attachment to their benefactors. There is reason to suspect that these protestations of loyalty proceed as much from hatred of the French party as from attachment to Great Britain, and no great dependence could be placed upon them in any emergency.

It is to be regretted that the local Government and the press, instead of trying to root out the feelings of hatred and jealousy subsisting between these two classes, and to produce more friendly relations between them, have inadvertently or wilfully aided rather to widen the breach. There are men among the coloured people equal in intelligence, wealth, and character to any of the white Creoles, and the Governor should extend to these men the enjoyment of the same social as well as of the same political rights. If these men are worthy to sit in the Council-Chamber, they are worthy also to sit at the Governor's table, and to be present with their families at the Governor's balls. These matters may appear trifling, but it is upon trifles that the peace of mixed communities often depends. Hitherto the Government have played into the hands of the French party, who, without abating their claims or renouncing their nationality, are ready to profit by every concession, and have treated the coloured people with neglect. The great ambition of both classes is to obtain admission to the Government-House balls; and while cards of invitation are lavishly distributed among the white Creoles, so that it is not unusual to see there shopkeepers' assistants, and others still less reputable, whose only claim to admission is their *pur sang*, the most distinguished families among the coloured population are excluded. The excuse for this exclusion is that, if the coloured people were invited, the whites would not come. We believe that the love of dancing among this class is stronger than their repugnance to colour; but, even if it were otherwise, it seems scarcely right to treat one part of the population with injustice in order to gratify the foolish prejudices of the other. Like the nation whose blood circulates in their veins, the coloured population are far more ambitious of social than of political equality, and it seems scarcely politic to wound the feelings of that portion of the community who profess attachment to British institutions, in deference to the absurd prejudices of those who treat them with ridicule and scorn. So long as the coloured people are excluded from Government House, their white neighbours will treat them as an inferior class, and subject them to the same social ostracism which they see practised by their Governors. Accordingly, the white Creole will meet the coloured one, in all matters of business, on a footing of equality, will sit with him in the Council-Chamber, and even associate with him as his partner in trade, but he would as soon think of asking him to his table as of conferring that honour upon a passenger by a cholera ship from India.

The press also, by the scurrilous articles which appear in its daily columns, keeps alive these prejudices, and profits by the evil passions which it fosters and excites. The organ of the French party, in which able articles occasionally appear, covers the coloured people with bitter sarcasms, which are all the more keenly felt, because they are sometimes true. The organ of the coloured people retaliates by foretelling the time when the degenerate descendants of the whites shall become the cooks and coachmen of the coloured men, and by appealing to the evil passions of the latter class. The English party have no organ, but the only gazette edited by an Englishman joins in the senseless cry against the coloured people, and treats them and their leaders with undisguised contempt. An instance of the good feeling shewn by the white Creole towards the coloured, and of the correct taste exhibited by an English editor, may be given, as a better indication of the state of manners than any general description. In 1857, a coloured man was chosen Mayor of Port Louis. There is a special box at the theatre set apart for the Mayor, when he appears there after his accession to office. A number of *jeunes gens* got hold of a negro, made him insensible with drink, clothed him in evening costume, with gloves and cravat complete, and placed him in this condition in the Mayor's box. His appearance there was the signal for a disgraceful riot, the whole blame of which rests with the white population. The English editor, instead of decrying the conduct of the young men who had thus wantonly insulted some sixty thousand of their fellow-citizens, treated the whole affair as an excellent joke. The coloured people failed to see it in this light, and one of their number committed an assault upon the editorial person, unjustifiable no doubt, but not more so than the cause which gave rise to it.

The Royal College is the only institution in the colony where the youth of both classes meet on a footing of equality, and have an opportunity of trying their intellectual strength. There can be no doubt but that the admiration, which the minds of the young feel for intellectual prowess, is stronger than the antipathy of colour, and that the honourable position which the coloured lads have attained there, by their talents and perseverance, has caused them to be regarded in a different light by those who formerly depreciated their abilities. Two of the best pupils are sent home every year to be educated at the expense of the Government, and each of these receives £200 per annum for that purpose. It is highly honourable to the coloured people, that during the last five or six years, all the pupils, with two exceptions, selected for this honour belonged to their number, and that the selection was grounded on superior merit alone. Most of them have

adopted the legal or medical profession, and some of
them have made a distinguished appearance when they
entered the lists with the young Anglo-Saxons, who
had every advantage of training. No money could be
better expended than that devoted to the education of
these young men. Besides exciting their gratitude, it
makes them familiar with the English language and
with English institutions, removes many foolish prejudices, teaches self-respect, and enables them to take
a position in society to which they could never have
otherwise aspired. Imbued with a feeling of deep
admiration for England, the *alma mater* that supplied
them with intellectual food, they spread this feeling
among their countrymen, and excite their wonder by
telling them of mountains loftier than the Pieter Both,
and of lakes larger than the Grand Basin. Their
superior intelligence makes them the leaders of their
party, and the influence thus acquired is employed in
increasing the feeling of attachment to the country
which has conferred upon them such advantages. The
benefits derived from this liberal grant are not confined
to the recipients. The parents of other young men are
induced to send their children home, that they may
receive the same education as the Government pupils;
and none but those who have witnessed the strong
feelings of affection existing between Creole parents and
their children, can appreciate this sacrifice of feeling to
duty. There can be no doubt but that the coloured
population are growing every year in intelligence and
wealth, and that they are more sincerely attached to

Great Britain than the other section of the Mauritius community. It is the duty, therefore, of the local Government to shew that they have no sympathy with the prejudice against them, and to admit them to the same social equality as the other class.

The standard of morality cannot be expected to be very high in a place where slavery has been recently abolished. The curse of slavery is not confined to the slave; it extends also to the slaveholder and his descendants for successive generations. Power uncontrolled by law, by moral principle, or by public opinion, must always have a deteriorating effect upon its possessor, as well as upon the victims on whom it is exercised. In the one it engenders violence and cruelty; in the other, meanness and falsehood. The children of the slaveholder add generally to the violence and cruelty of their parent, the meanness, the dishonesty, and the falsehood of his slaves. The coloured population, who are descended partly from slaveholders and from slaves, share in those vices, which are, in a good measure, the result of their peculiar position. They are not worse, perhaps, than the whites, but they might be much better, without being over-righteous. Vice does not obtrude itself so much on public notice, or shew such a shameless face in the streets of Port Louis, as in those of some of our large towns at home; but the most decent cities are often the most dissolute. The absence of vice from the streets is generally a proof that vice, instead of being an excrescence, forms part of the system, discernible everywhere beneath the surface. Those familiar with

Continental or Eastern life will admit this truth, though at first sight it appears paradoxical. The marriage relation, formerly little regarded, and still easily dissolved, is now more generally observed; and it argues something for an improving tone of morality among the English part of the community, that young men known to have contracted one of those disgraceful connexions, once so rife in this colony as to form part of its *mœurs*, are excluded from society, and obliged to associate with others in the same lapsed condition.

The soil of Mauritius is not favourable to the growth of truthfulness of character, and the coloured people are accused by the white Creoles of being specially blameworthy in this respect. The Englishman, however, who has sat in a Mauritius court of justice, and listened to the wholesale perjury, and undisguised contempt for the sacred nature of an oath, exhibited by the Creoles of all classes, will be reminded, perhaps, of the old Latin proverb about Clodius, and be disposed to regard falsehood as a vice common to the whole Creole community, instead of being the characteristic of the coloured people. "There is not a coloured man in the colony who would not perjure himself for a sixpence," is the frequent charge brought against this class by the white Creoles, whom the consciousness of their own defects might teach a little charity. Time, education, a purer form of religion, and intercourse with Englishman, who, whatever their other faults may be, despise lying as the meanest of all vices, will do much to correct this evil habit.

The better class of coloured women have slender, graceful, elegant figures, sparkling black eyes, and delicate, finely-cut features, with abundance of dark wavy hair, of which they are extremely vain. They are passionately fond of dress, and willingly submit to any privation throughout the year to be enabled to appear at the races in the gayest silks that the looms of Lyons can produce. Marriages between them and Englishmen of the lower class are not unfrequent, and they seem to be faithful wives and affectionate mothers. It is only of late years that female education has begun to make progress among this class; and it must be admitted that far more attention is paid to the cultivation of outward graces, than to imparting a sound and useful education. Music is an accomplishment cultivated among all ranks; and while the coloured women have naturally fine voices, they are too apt to mistake strength for skill, and howling for harmony. Every house in Port Louis, however poor, seems to possess a piano. It appears to be the mark of respectability, like Thurtell's gig. It may be an old ricketty tumble-down thing, with half its chords in a state of collapse, and rheumatism in every joint. It may be less harmonious than an Indian tomtom or a Chinese gong. It may have seen service for successive generations, and Virginia even may have discoursed on it in the days of La Bourdonnais. White ants may have hollowed out tunnels in its inward recesses, and left it scarcely a leg to stand upon. No matter. So long as it can stand or totter on its legs, it is still a piano, and a pledge of respectability. It forms part of the dowry of Ambroisine, who bequeaths it to Artémise or Angeline, her first-born, who treasures it as a mark of past and present respectability. Good society must draw the line somewhere, and in Mauritius it does not extend its circle beyond a piano. Every family with a piano is respectable; and as almost every family wishes to be respectable, almost every family has a piano. The noise that is made by these tinking old impostures, especially in the evening, when that noise is accompanied with the howling of all the dogs in the neighbourhood, whose nervous system it seems to affect unpleasantly, might form an appropriate concert at a witches' sabbath. I may áppear to write strongly on this subject, but I had the misfortune to live two months in a house where I was surrounded by musical neighbours; and really I would not wish my greatest enemy a worse punishment than to be located two months in the same locality. It is related of Theodore Hook, of witty but somewhat disreputable memory, whose disease of the chest was caught in the Mauritius, that, excited one night to frenzy by the howling of a dog, the tinkling of a piano, and the voice of a dusky syren, in a neighbouring compound, he rushed into the house and declared that he would eat up dog, piano, and all, if they did not stop the dreadful noise.

The white Creole population of French descent represents almost all the different elements that compose European society. It is composed of the descendants of the husbandmen from Bourbon and the pirates from

Madagascar, who took possession of the island after the departure of the Dutch—of the officers, soldiers, and sailors, connected with the French East India Company, who settled in the colony—of the old *noblesse* who found refuge there, after having lost their all in the French Revolution—and of adventurers of different professions, who, being better known than trusted in Europe, found an asylum and a field for the exercise of their talents in Mauritius. It took many years before elements so diverse could amalgamate, so as to present the settled form which society has now assumed. The more peaceful of the inhabitants suffered severely from the military license of the soldiers sent from France, many of whom were desperadoes who had been guilty of crimes of the deepest dye at home, and who often murdered one another with their bayonets on the smallest provocation. The officers, in some cases, seem to have been little superior to the men whom they commanded. A French colonel having met with a repulse from a planter's wife, employed one of his men to burn the planter's house and all its inmates, during his absence. This horrid villany was actually perpetrated, and the assassin detected and executed; but the officer who had employed him was beyond the reach of the law. This was not the last act of the tragedy. The planter, on his return, finding all his earthly happiness wrecked, challenged the murderer of his family, and fell by his hand. Such a crime could never have been committed by a British officer, or been allowed to pass unpunished by British law.

The first settlers were, as at the present day, engaged in mercantile pursuits, or employed in the cultivation of the soil. The island became a sort of *entrepôt* for the trade between India and Europe; and the merchants, enjoying a sort of monopoly, exacted more for European goods than they could be sold at in India, and made Indian goods dearer than in Europe—a state of things which continues till the present day. The planters were engaged in the cultivation of indigo, cotton, and sugar, but apparently with little success. Baron Grant, writing in 1746, mentions that the different undertakings for raising cotton and indigo had failed. One sugar plantation had in some measure succeeded. It produced a sugar resembling the coarser honey of Europe, which was sold at two sous per lb. The more wealthy adventurers were absolutely starving, from having been compelled to purchase provisions for themselves and their slaves, for whom they had no adequate means of support. Who, on looking at this picture, could recognise Mauritius of the present day?

The description given by St. Pierre of the character and morals of the planters and merchants of this island is very unfavourable. He describes them as destitute of every feeling of honour, probity, or humanity, of all taste for literature or the fine arts, and as living in utter neglect of those domestic institutions on which the peace and happiness of every community depend. The character ascribed by him to the women is far more pleasing. There were about four hundred planters and one hundred women of condition in the colony. The latter resided principally on the estates, and rarely visited the town, except at Easter for confession, or on the occasion of a ball. Like their descendants, they were passionately fond of dress, and glad of every opportunity of breaking the dull monotony of their existence. They were sober, temperate, devoted to their children, lively and pleasing in their manners, and more virtuous than might have been expected in such a state of society. Admiral Kempenfelt describes them as fond of constant exercise, and bold equestrians—accomplishments which their fair descendants assuredly do not possess. In beauty and elegance of shape he held them superior to their countrywomen in France, but they were inferior in point of education, some of them being so ignorant that they could not even read. When they went abroad they were carried in palanquins, each of which was borne by eight slaves. The use of carriages was almost unknown; there was only one in the colony when it was captured by the English. Palanquins have now been superseded by the elegant vehicles of Jones; it is found more economical to keep two large horses than to feed eight slaves. The appearance of a palanquin borne by eight persons would excite as much sensation in the streets of Port Louis at the present day, as that of a sedan-chair borne by two venerable chairmen in the streets of London.

The white Creole population of Mauritius may be divided into two classes—the planters, and the inhabitants of Port Louis. The planters are generally a fine, frank, hospitable race, passionately fond of field-sports, and possessed of great physical strength. From their constant exposure to the open air, and their active habits, they have suffered less from the influences of the climate than the inhabitants of Port Louis, and may well bear comparison with the strongest and healthiest of their kinsmen in France. There is much of the simplicity of early patriarchal times in their mode of life. Often there are four or five families living on the same estate, all bound together by the closest ties; and, though occupying different pavilions or cottages, meeting together daily, and dining at the same common table. A rude hospitality is exercised to all comers, and the Englishman who has tact enough to enter into their feelings, and to make some allowance for their prejudices, is always sure to be welcome. While they have retained their nationality, and identify themselves in feeling and habits with the old country, they are not insensible to the advantages which they enjoy under the British flag, and there is perhaps more of bravado than sincerity in their often-expressed desire to be reunited to France. If an attempt should ever be made to effect this reunion, the most dangerous class would be the planters. Accustomed from childhood to the use of fire-arms, acquainted with every pass where a stand could be made, hardy, vigorous, and capable of enduring great bodily fatigue, the planters would be a much more formidable foe than the degenerate race that throngs the streets of Port Louis. So long, however, as England retains the supremacy at sea, no attempt at insurrection in Mauritius can be permanently successful, and no worse consequence is likely to ensue from a popular outbreak, than the coercion or intimidation of a weak or vacillating Governor. The large sum received by the planters in compensation for the loss which they sustained by the emancipation of their slaves, enabled them for a time to indulge in the most reckless expenditure, and led to the formation of habits which ultimately involved them in great distress, and in many cases compelled them to sell their estates, which fell into the hands of a different class. Those who have been able to retain them are scarcely ever free from debt, and the capitalists who advance them money exact such an exorbitant interest, that their victims have little chance of ever escaping from their power. Usury is the vulture that is preying upon the vitals of Mauritius society.

The Creoles of Port Louis differ very much in appearance and character from the hardy, active planters. They live, as it were, in a different climate. There is a difference of fifteen degrees between the temperature of Port Louis, where the heat during six months of the year is most oppressive, and that of Moka and other country districts. The effect of this difference upon the human frame is perceptible in the appearance of the inhabitants of Port Louis. They do not possess the same bodily strength, or the same mental energy, as the *habitans*. The effects of the heat are visible in their attenuated forms and pale languid faces. The immoderate use of tobacco, with the odour of which the atmosphere of Port Louis is constantly impregnated, adds to the enervating influences of the climate, and aids in producing that indolent listlessness of appearance with which strangers are so much struck. The natural vivacity of the French character seems to have evaporated, and to have given place to a general indifference to every thing except the dread of cholera, which occasionally produces a sort of temporary insanity. They share in the same defects of character, and are marked by the same vices as the coloured population. Truth and honesty have few admirers, and the man of genius is the smart man, in the American sense of the term. Few of them have ever left their native isle; many of them have scarcely ever been beyond the bounds of the muncipality; and a trip to Bourbon is a feat that is seldom attempted. The effect of their being cribbed and confined within such narrow limits is, that their mental vision becomes equally circumscribed, and that they are literally little better than children of a larger growth, " pleased with a rattle, tickled with a straw." They are not deficient in natural abilities, but they have no field for their exercise, and their minds are too often seriously occupied with trifles unworthy of their notice. A friend related to me that he spent an evening in the society of some young Creoles of the better class. The whole conversation was occupied with the consideration of the important question, whether it was better to wear straps or to dispense with them as an appendage of dress. One cannot be long in their society without being struck with the narrowness of their views and the littleness of their minds. Those who have been educated in Europe for the bar or the medical profession, have of course more enlarged and liberal views, and some of the most amiable and intelligent members of Mauritius society are to be found in the ranks of these two professions. Their residence in a temperate climate during the period of youth seems to have had an expanding influence upon their bodies as well as their minds, they being in many cases as superior to their countrymen in physical organisation as in mental prowess. The advantages of home education are now more felt, and a greater number of Creole youths are sent to Europe for their education than used to be in former years.

The shopkeepers of Port Louis are a singular class. They have nothing of that obsequiousness, or anxiety to please, which distinguishes those engaged in the same business in Europe. Each one seems to feel that his shop is his castle, and that an apology is due to him from every customer who takes the liberty of entering. In Europe, a customer thinks that, in buying from a shopkeeper, there is a mutual benefit to the buyer and the seller, but the Mauritius shopkeeper practically dissents from this theory of reciprocity. He thinks that all the benefit is on the side of the buyer, and is at no pains to conceal his opinion. When a customer enters, he continues quietly smoking his cigar, and stares vacantly at the intruder. The demand for any article leads him apparently to take a mental review of all his goods before he ventures on an answer. That answer is generally in the negative. If the customer points out the article, which he is too lazy to look for, he shews his gratitude by demanding four times its value. He prices his goods, not by their intrinsic value, but by the apparent necessities of the purchaser, and even when he gets the price he demands, he drops the money listlessly into the till, with the general air of a man who has been rather ill-used in the transaction, and whose dignity has been in some measure compromised. The best way to do shopping pleasantly is to approach the shopkeeper as if he were really some great person, to exhibit towards him all those exaggerated forms of politeness, which even the negroes have picked up, to engage him in general conversation, and, at a convenient opportunity, to mention casually that you require such an article, and that you would feel infinitely obliged to any one who could supply you with it. The shopkeeper, in a friendly way, produces the article, and marks his sense of your politeness by exacting sixty instead of a hundred per cent. of profit. If you wound his *amour propre*, he will avenge himself upon your purse. It is a striking and significant fact, that the Jews, who have overrun all the great cities of the East, and monopolised certain branches of trade, have never been able to gain a footing in Mauritius. They found the field already occupied by a class who had mastered the art of usury in all its details, and whom they could teach nothing in the practice of unprincipled exaction. The colony has gained an unenviable notoriety in the commercial world ; and the disclosure of some of the commercial transactions of the last half century would redound little to its honour. That task must be left to some abler and more practised hand; but a stranger cannot but be struck with the laxity of principle and utter disregard of truth, and of the sacred nature of an oath, evinced by the Creoles. Perjury is so common in the courts of justice that it excites little notice, and recently a leading member of the bar announced, in open court, the rather startling principle in ethics, that perjury was no longer perjury when used by a son to screen his father from punishment. Something has been done of late years to purify the bar, and to produce a healthier tone among its members; but the Hercules who undertook the task found himself unable to cleanse this Augean stable from the moral pollution which had accumulated in it for more than a century. The Mauritians know when and how to give a sop to Cerberus.

The simplicity of manners and dress attributed to the Creole ladies by the early writers, is now unknown. They no longer walk to the bazaar in the morning dressed in light muslin, and wearing no other covering for the head than that which nature has bestowed. Negresses and women of colour may be seen occasionally in this dress and *coiffure;* but the Creole ladies never venture out except in carriages for the morning and evening drive. The simple costume worn in the days of Virginia has been discarded for the most recent *modes* from Paris, and the fair Creoles of Mauritius can scarcely be distinguished from their fair kinswomen of France, save by that *morbidezza*—that elegant languor of expression—which is all their own, and which has gained much admiration for those amongst them who have appeared in Parisian society. " The ladies of the Isle of France," says Laplace,* " enjoy a just reputation for beauty, both in Europe and the Indies ; they are pretty and graceful, with charming figures ; their disposition is lively and gay, which is in some cases joined to a careful education." Those of them who have been educated in Europe, are admired for their graceful and attractive manners. The natural vivacity of the French character is sobered by the effects of climate, and their minds enlarged by mingling with European society. They are passionately attached to their sunny, romantic isle, and long for it amid all the fascinations of European society. The Englishmen who have intermarried with them have rarely been able to leave the island, or if they have, they experienced much difficulty in persuading their wives to accompany them. Cases have occurred when they yielded only at the last moment, when the vessel which was to convey them to Europe had unfurled her sails. Then they tore themselves from their beloved isle, with much the same feelings as those attributed by Beranger to Mary Stuart, on leaving France. A few have married officers, belonging to regiments stationed in the colony ; but these cases are very rare. Marriage in Mauritius is a very complicated affair in the case of strangers. The intending Benedict must procure seven witnesses, ready to swear that to their knowledge he is a single man. As the Mauritians are ready to swear to any-

* " Voyage autour du Monde."

thing, he has no difficulty in finding witnesses. On the principle of compensation, perhaps, the marriage tie is easily dissolved. By the French law, as set forth by the Code Napoleon, any married couple, dissatisfied with their condition, and finding themselves neither one nor two, can regain their liberty, by appearing before a magistrate, and declaring that they wish to be separated, on the ground of unsuitable dispositions (*incompatibilité d'humeur*). The magistrate receives their declaration, and remands them for twelve months. If they find themselves incorrigible, and repeat their declaration, they are then formally released from all claim or tie upon each other. The wife resumes her maiden name, and the husband, like Tony Lumpkin, is " his own man again." They are at liberty to marry again, if so disposed, and occasionally a man marries his own wife. Montgomery Martin remarks on this point—— " Divorces are frequent, although the marriage rites are performed with great ceremony, during which bets are often made as to how long the nuptial tie will remain unbroken. I was at one table in the island where two divorced wives were guests of the third consort of their former spouse, and there was much harmony and glee at the entertainment." Such cases, however, are now rare. Most Creoles are satisfied with one wife, a few more daring spirits venture on two, but I know of only one who has three.

The lives of the Creole ladies must be very monotonous, except during the gay season, which is opened by the ball given on the Queen's birth-day at Government

House. After this the garrison and masonic balls follow in rapid succession, and for a period of several
months, they have an opportunity of indulging their
taste for dancing and dress. While the priests have
obtained a stronger hold over them than over their
more sceptical husbands and brothers, when the bishop
excommunicated the Free-masons, the event proved
that their passion for dancing was stronger than their
dread of the Church's displeasure. It was dreadful, no
doubt, to imperil their souls ; but then the masonic
balls were charming—and, *enfin*, they could not but
dance. And they *did* dance, in defiance of Popish
bulls and priestly restrictions. The poorer families are
said to subject themselves to many privations throughout the year, that Adèle, Eugènie, and the other unmarried daughters of the house, may make a distinguished
appearance during the gay season.

The British population, besides the military, consists
of the Government *employés*, of about thirty merchants,
four or five planters, the professors of the Royal College,
the Government-school teachers, and a considerable number of old soldiers, who have left the service and settled
in the colony in different capacities. Many of the last
class have married coloured wives and become almost
identified with the coloured population. The British
residents of the better class form a small community by
themselves, and no one who has lived amongst them
and enjoyed their warm-hearted hospitality, can look
back to his intercourse with them without feelings of
unmingled pleasure. Most of them reside in the

Plaines Wilhelmes and Moka districts, and some of their country-houses are furnished with elegance and surrounded with every comfort. Most of them have received a liberal education, have seen much of the world, and are possessed of polished manners and great warmth of heart. Any case of real distress is sure to excite their warm sympathy, and to call forth their liberal assistance. Their comparative disregard of religious ordinances is, in a great measure, the result of the unfavourable circumstances in which they have been placed, and of late there has been a marked improvement in this respect. A few Creole families mingle freely in English society; but, as a general rule, the two classes keep aloof from one another. Various causes have been assigned for this coolness. It does not appear that the *entente cordiale* ever prevailed to a large extent, and it is not probable, so long as the colony remains French in feeling, language, and habits, that it ever will. The Creoles have all the susceptibility of a people whose vanity has been wounded by the imposition of a foreign yoke. When they feel themselves aggrieved, their usual cry is, "Nous sommes un peuple vaincu." They forget that Great Britain has never treated them as a conquered people ; that under her flag they have attained a degree of material prosperity to which they could never have otherwise aspired; and that it is their own fault if the position of the island is not eventually the same as that of any other British colony. The terms agreed upon at the capitulation of the island have been strictly observed, and they enjoy a larger amount of personal and political liberty than they ever possessed before that event. Their property and rights have been respected, and if their national susceptibility had been too acute to allow them to live beneath the British flag, the island of Bourbon lay at a convenient distance. It would have been easy to transport themselves, with their families, to that colony of France, and thus retain their connexion with the mother-country. If Mauritius had been an English colony conquered by France, a system of repression would have been adopted that would have trodden out all the remains of a lingering nationality, and in less than half a century assimilated the island to any other French colony. England has pursued an opposite course. She has fostered national prejudices and passions, and shewed an undue leaning in favour of the French party, till Mauritius has become the *enfant gâté* among her colonies, dissatisfied it knows not why, and aspiring to something it knows not what.

There was nothing in the capitulation of the island dishonourable to French courage. The soldiers could point proudly to their eagles, and say, "Vous n'avez pas pris nos petits martins." It was simply the yielding of an inferior to a superior force, and two honourable courses remained for the inhabitants—either to sell their property and remove to another French colony, or to make a virtue of necessity, and identify themselves with the conquering people, after the peace between France and England, when all hope of being restored to the mother-country was cut off. They have adopted neither of these courses. They have remained in the colony, under the protection of the British flag, and yet they openly avow their hatred and contempt for British institutions and manners. Mauritius is in feeling, manners, and almost in language, as much a French colony as it was fifty years ago, and every Englishman resident in it feels himself a foreigner in a British colony.

After the capture of the island, before there was a press to act as a safety-valve for national susceptibility, it found vent through the medium of frequent challenges sent to the British officers and residents. The Champ de Mars was the field of contest, and these hostile meetings were of frequent occurrence, till one of the governors, an earnest, practical man, put down duelling, by banishing the combatants from the island, without inquiring into the merits of the case. This summary procedure had the desired effect; and for some years back there has been only one hostile meeting, the principals in which were rival editors. There was more ink than blood spilt on the occasion. Their pens were sharper than their swords.

Other causes besides wounded national vanity have led to the separation which at present exists between French and English society. The intercourse between these two classes seems to have been more frequent and familiar before the abolition of slavery—a measure which excited the bitterest opposition in the colony, and was regarded as the prelude to its ruin. As physical resistance to this measure was impossible, the Creoles avenged themselves by expelling the English and their partisans from their *coteries*. The latter resented this conduct by establishing an exclusiveness as stringent as that of the Creole party, and thus there resulted an estrangement of feeling, which, heightened and increased by other causes, has not yet died out. The local press, instead of trying to bridge over the gulf that separates the two parties, and to produce more amicable relations between them, profited by this dissension. In such a small community there are few topics of much interest for the press to discuss, beyond the current price of Cheddar cheeses, and other articles of produce or consumption, and yet there are four daily papers, each of which has its editorial leaders. As there are few local subjects to afford the material for the construction of these leaders, the editors find a never-failing resource in appealing to old prejudices, in lamenting the loss of nationality, and in pouring contempt upon the manners and institutions of the British. The press of Mauritius has had more to do in fostering bad passions, and in keeping alive the slumbering embers of national antipathy between the two classes, than any other cause. It has trafficked in and made merchandise of feelings which, in the natural course of things, would soon have died out. To serve its own selfish ends, it has pandered to popular passions and prejudices, and kept open a festering sore, that might otherwise have healed up. It has mistaken licentiousness for liberty, and overstepped those bounds which public opinion has, in all free countries, drawn around the sacred precincts of private life. In all enlightened communities, public opinion is an effectual check upon the licentiousness of the press; and the press of every country may always be regarded as an indication of the character of the people. Judged by this test, the character of the people of Mauritius cannot appear in a favourable light to other communities; and there can be no doubt but that the press has produced a strong impression against them at home. The liberty of the press can only be an advantage in communities where an enlightened public opinion will serve as a check to prevent it from degenerating into licentiousness. In Mauritius there is no public opinion, and if the Home Government were to impose a censorship on the Mauritius press, similar to that which is established in Bourbon, they would confer a boon which would be productive of the best effects, and be hailed as a blessing by the more enlightened members of society.

The attempt to implant British institutions—the slow growth of centuries—in the Mauritius soil, has been an utter failure. In this island they have no more life or vitality than the leafless poles known in France as trees of liberty, and have as much resemblance to the parent institutions as these poles have to real trees. These institutions have sprung up naturally on the British soil, but they cannot be transplanted to the tropics. The Town Council of Port Louis, an institution of recent creation, has fallen into merited contempt, and it is almost impossible to induce any respectable person to accept a seat in it. Instead of trying to introduce better sanitary arrangements into the town of Port Louis, it sets itself up as a rival institution to the local Government, and endeavours to act the same part as the Municipality of Paris in the first French Revolution. Trial by jury is the only other British institution yet introduced, and its working may lead the Home Government to hesitate before attempting any other experiment. When the intelligent jurymen, on whose fiat sometimes depends the life of a fellow-being, cannot arrive at unanimity, it is not unusual to appeal to chance or fate for the final decision. This appeal is made in the same way as that practised by our " city Arabs" with the copper coins which their industry has enabled them to collect. Comment upon such a fact is unnecessary.

There may be some future period when the spread of education, the extinction of national antipathies, the establishment of a purer form of religion, and the legitimate influence exercised by a well-regulated press, shall entitle Mauritius to a larger amount of self-government, and fit her for the reception of British institutions and the exercise of British rights; but her best friends must admit that that period has not yet arrived ; and any attempt to anticipate its arrival by the premature introduction of organic changes, foreign to the habits and feelings of the people, can end only in failure and disappointment. The paternal mode of government, firmly but mildly administered, as in the neighbouring island of Bourbon, is the one best adapted to Mauritius in her present condition.

CHAPTER IV.

Supposed Healthiness of Mauritius—Quarantine—Want of Cleanliness —Increase of Population—Cholera foretold in 1851—Absence of Hurricanes—Cholera in 1854—First Outbreak in the Civil Prison— The *Sultany*—Erratic Course of Cholera—Drunkards and Chinamen Escape—Strange Cause Assigned for Cholera—Panic in Port Louis —Cholera Contagious—Second Outbreak at Flacq—Its Cause— Massacre of Coolies on Flat Island—Second Outbreak of Cholera in 1856—Licentiousness of the Press—Arrival of the *Shah Jehan*— Mob at Government House—The *Friend of India*—Suspension of Coolie Emigration—Increase of Disease in Mauritius—Influence of Climate—Monotony of Life the Cause of Disease—The Remedy.

MAURITIUS long bore the reputation of being one of the healthiest spots in the world. Isolated, as it were, from the rest of the world, and fanned continually by the healthy sea breeze, it was long believed to be exempt from those pestilential diseases which seem to find their appropriate home in the East, though latterly they have forced their way to almost every part of the globe. The ravages made by cholera in 1819 left in the minds of the Mauritians a strong feeling of terror against a second inroad of this pestilence, and as it was firmly believed that it had been introduced by an English vessel called the *Topaz*, they insisted upon the Government adopting a stringent system of quarantine, which proved very annoying to vessels from India, the crews of which seldom escape without a few cases of diarrhœa, which the fears of the Mauritians were ever ready to magnify into Asiatic cholera. As there was no decided outbreak of cholera from 1819 to 1854 (although there is reason to believe that sporadic cases have always existed), the enforcement of the quarantine laws had become less strict, and the inhabitants had fallen into such a state of false security as to neglect even those ordinary conditions, the observance of which is considered in all civilised countries essential to the preservation of health. While there are perhaps a thousand carriages in Port Louis, the houses are destitute of all those conveniences which an Englishman regards as essential to the enjoyment of health. The gutters are uncovered, and the poorer inhabitants are in the habit of emptying their refuse into them. The effect of a tropical sun, whose scorching rays have raised the temperature to 90° in the shade, upon these open gutters, can neither be conceived nor realised, except by actual experience. The exorbitant sums exacted as house rent have led the inhabitants of Port Louis to crowd themselves into smaller space than can be beneficial either to their health or their morals. It is not unusual to find five or six families occupying a house which in England would barely accommodate one. The Asiatics have carried this system of crowding to a greater excess than the Creoles. A single room serves the same purpose to them as a single house to the Creoles. Five or six Indian families may be found, in the neighbourhood of the bazaar, occupying a room of such limited dimensions, as scarcely to leave sufficient space for their recumbent bodies, and the stifling atmosphere is impregnated with the intoxicating fumes of gandia, to which the miserable inmates have had recourse to superinduce a temporary oblivion. In the larger and more frequented streets, there is a certain attempt at cleanliness and decency, but the smaller lanes are reeking with noxious exhalations, which, in the rainy season, carry death and desolation to the homes of the surrounding population. In the neighbourhood of the Trou Fanfaron, at low water, there are such noxious odours and pestilential exhalations from the filth that has been allowed to accumulate in the harbour, that the inhabitants of that quarter, accustomed from their infancy to breathe a tainted atmosphere, are sometimes obliged, in self-defence, to close their doors and windows. The inhabitants of Port Louis, at the present day, are probably not less cleanly in their habits than their predecessors; but it is acknowledged on all hands that the town has become much more unhealthy in the course of the last twenty years. The inhabitants ascribe this increasing unhealthiness to the influx of Indian immigrants, who, they affirm, bring with them the fevers of India. There can be no doubt but that disease has been much more frequent and intense of late years; but the principal cause of this is to be found in the rapid increase of the population, and the neglect of the sanitary conditions which such an increase rendered necessary for the preservation of health. When the population of the town was smaller and more widely scattered, the miasmatic influences proceeding from the causes to which we have alluded, being spread over a larger surface, were less violent in their effects; but from the increase of the population, without a corresponding increase of houses for their accommodation, and the neglect of ordinary sanitary conditions, these miasmatic influences have grown in intensity and power, and have made fevers, and other complaints formerly unknown, endemic.

These remarks are intended to shew that there were predisposing influences to cholera at work before the actual outbreak of 1854. These influences were so well known to intelligent medical men, who did not hold the contagion theory, but believed that cholera might arise from a tainted condition of the atmosphere, superinduced by the violation of sanitary laws, that some of them expressed their surprise that Mauritius should have been so long exempt from cholera, and their conviction that a fearful outbreak of that pestilence might soon be expected. This conviction was announced with prophetic truth by Dr Mouat, an intelligent officer belonging to the Bengal medical staff, who visited the colony, and published a small work upon it and the neighbouring island of Bourbon, in 1851. This announcement met with about as much credence from the Mauritians, as the prophecies of Cassandra from the sons and daughters of Priam. They shrugged their shoulders, and characterised him as "un brave homme, mais tant soit peu fou," pointing expressively to their foreheads. They looked upon him with much the same feelings of surprise, pity, and ridicule, as the antediluvians may be supposed to have regarded Noah when he preached a deluge and began to build an ark. And when at length the sweeping pestilence came, it found a population, physically and morally, as unfit to resist its ravages, as the contemporaries of Noah to stem the waters of the deluge. The writer of these pages has no other object in view than to give a slight sketch of the appearance which things presented during cholera in 1854. He has no theory of contagion or of non-contagion to combat or to advocate. He believes that, without adopting the theory of contagion, there were sufficient local causes at work to account for the outbreak of cholera. He admits that, both in 1854 and 1856, there were facts that came under his personal observation that could scarcely be accounted for without the admission that cholera is in certain cases contagious.

There is a circumstance worthy of remark, although at first sight it may appear to have but little connexion with the question of cholera. Of late years hurricanes have been of much less frequent occurrence at Mauritius than formerly. While different causes have been assigned for this circumstance, the fact itself is indisputable. It is now nearly twelve years since a hurricane worthy of the name has visited Mauritius. The latter months of summer seldom pass away without being accompanied with strong gales, which the members of the Meteorological Society define as the last dying gasps of some monster hurricane. But of late years the colony has experienced none of those sweeping hurricanes, which formerly proved so destructive to life and property, and of whose power such questionable stories are related. The absence of these hurricanes can scarcely be regarded as an unmingled blessing. While attended with much temporary inconvenience and considerable loss, they had the immediate effect of sweeping away all the noxious vapours and exhalations that accumulated in the atmosphere, and sometimes for successive days impended over Port Louis, in the shape of dark clouds, when no breath of air was stirring, and the temperature was that of a heated oven. While it was found that the health of the community suffered before the advent of a hurricane, a decided improvement was always experienced after its departure. Like similar outbursts in the moral world, it purified the atmosphere, and though devastating in its first effects, proved ultimately a blessing. The cause of the breaking out of cholera in 1854 may be traced perhaps (for on such a question, still *sub judice*, it would be folly to dogmatise) neither to contagion from the introduction of diseased Coolies, nor to intercourse between the *Sultany* and the fishermen of the coast, but to the accumulation of noxious vapours and gases in the atmosphere, from the decaying animal and vegetable matter festering in the streets and lanes of Port Louis, and the want of a good rattling hurricane to sweep these vapours and gases away, and thus purify the atmosphere. Before searching for the *quid divinum* as the cause of any public calamity, we ought to look first whether some *quid humanum* may not be found sufficient to account for its occurrence. If it be objected that Port Louis had continued many years in the same sanitary condition, without an outbreak of cholera, it must be borne in mind that of late years there has been a rapid increase of population, without any effort being made to provide for their personal cleanliness and health, and that experience in similar cases shews that when the blow is delayed it falls the more heavily when it descends.

From 1819 to 1854 Mauritius was exempt from cholera, or if isolated cases occasionally occurred, they were not of a violent character, and were passed over in silence. The island enjoyed a high reputation in Europe for the salubrity of its climate, the purity of its atmosphere, and the absence of many of those causes that make life in the East unpleasant. It was occasionally visited by invalids from Europe and India, the former desirous to escape from the severity of a northern winter, the latter from the scorching sun of an Indian summer. But this high reputation was not to extend beyond 1854. The population, sunk in their ordinary apathy and carelessness, heard with incredulous indifference that isolated cases of cholera had occurred from the beginning of the year. It was only towards the middle of May that they were roused from their state of security by the undeniable proof that cholera was in the midst of them.

We propose to present a simple statement of the facts of the case, derived partly from personal ob-

servation and the Report of the Committee appointed
by Government to investigate the origin of the disease.
The Committee entered on their arduous task in
August 1854, and published the result of their labours
in a Report, which is valuable only from the facts it
contains, and interesting only from the different impressions produced by these facts on the minds of
medical men. It was believed at first, that cholera
manifested the first symptoms of its presence among
the prisoners detained in the jail of Port Louis. The
jail is a large, ill-ventilated building, situated in the
centre of the town. In the month of May 1854, it
was overcrowded with Indian vagabonds, heaped together without much regard to space, cleanliness, or
the means of respiration. The acting Governor,
moved by the complaints of the planters against the
remissness of the police in endeavouring to suppress
the system of *marronage* among their Indian labourers,
commenced a *razzia* against all Indians found wandering in the fields or streets who could not give an
account of themselves ; and soon filled the jail with
men emaciated with want, and therefore predisposed to
disease. On the 14th of May, cholera broke out in the
jail, and its first victim was a Creole of the name of
Emilien. The press, which had lauded the efforts of the
acting Governor to second the wishes of the planters, was
now as loud in denouncing them, and did not scruple
to ascribe the outbreak of cholera to his ill-timed zeal.
Subsequent research, however, has sufficiently shewn
that there were already isolated cases in the colony, and

that there must have been predisposing causes in the atmosphere, before the overcrowding of the civil prisons and the subsequent outbreak of cholera took place.

The only question of interest, so far as regards the theory of contagion, that presents itself here, is whether cholera existed in the colony previous to the arrival of the *Sultany*, a vessel from Calcutta, loaded with Coolies, which arrived in the harbour of Port Louis on the 24th of March. She had left Calcutta on the 14th of February. Thirteen days after her departure, cholera broke out on board, and during the passage she lost thirty men. On the 25th of March, the day after her arrival, the Chief Medical Officer reported the existence of the disease to the authorities, and requested the removal of the infected vessel. The letter was forwarded to the Harbour-master, with the request to take the necessary steps to give effect to this recommendation. From causes unknown to us, the vessel remained in the harbour till the 30th of March, when the Board of Health met, and ordered the Coolies to be disembarked at Flat Island. But nothing had been prepared for their reception, and it was only on the 7th of April that the *Sultany* left the harbour. In the interval of fourteen days, which elapsed between her arrival and departure, five new cases of cholera occurred on board. The *Sultany* disembarked her immigrants on the 9th of April, and returned to the Bell buoy on the 11th, and received *pratique* on the 19th of April. The Coolies disembarked at Flat Island soon regained their health. Only three deaths occurred, and none of these from cholera. The quarantine was raised on the 1st of May, and so fully convinced was the Board of Health of the non-contagiousness of cholera, that they decided that there was no necessity for destroying the clothes which the immigrants had worn during the passage. The clothes could have been of no great value in a pecuniary point of view, and a small sum of money would have been sufficient to indemnify the owners ; but the Board of Health no doubt wished, even in the smallest things, to act consistently with their own convictions.

A strong effort has been made by the contagionists to shew that the outbreak of cholera followed immediately on the arrival of the *Sultany*, and that there were no cases in Port Louis before that event. The existence of such cases is now, however, fully recognised. A man of the name of Bonin died on the 2d of. January, of the worst kind of Asiatic cholera. On the 18th of January and the 26th of February, two soldiers of the 85th Regiment were attacked, and subsequently recovered. Two other cases occurred at Pamplemousses, and two at Black River, with what result we cannot tell. These facts prove that there was cholera, no matter by what technical name it may be designated, in Port Louis, before the arrival of the *Sultany*, and render it impossible to establish a causal connexion between these two events. To do so, it would be necessary to shew that there were no cases of cholera in Port Louis before the general outbreak, and even if this were demonstrated (which cannot be done), the con-

nexion between the two events might still be merely a
coincidence in point of time.   The *Sultany*, it will be
remembered, arrived on the 24th of March.   No case
of cholera occurred till the 10th of April, when an ex-
apprentice (or old slave), and a child of five years of
age, died in Desforges Street.   An interval of seventeen
days thus elapsed between the arrival of the *Sultany*
and the occurrence of the first isolated case of cholera.
On the 15th of April, a washerwoman was attacked,
and on the 16th, two Creole carpenters, one of whom
died.   On the 6th of May, the child of one Malfait died
at Grand River.   On the 7th, the aunt of the child,
who had nursed it, was attacked, and died on the 8th.
Particular attention is requested to the date of this
woman's death, as much weight has been attached to it.
On the 12th of May, two fishermen died at Grand
River, and on the same day, a female servant in Port
Louis.   On the 14th, cholera broke out in the civil
prison, overcrowded with Indian vagabonds.   Its spread
among these poor wretches was very rapid.   On the
15th of May, there were eleven cases; on the 16th,
seventeen cases; on the 17th, twenty cases; on the 18th,
eight cases; on the 19th, three cases; and two on the
21st—in all fifty cases in the course of seven days.
The remainder of the prisoners who had escaped from
this fiery trial were then dispersed in different quarters,
some being sent to other prisons, others to an old hulk
belonging to the Messrs Blythe, and the rest to Flat
Island.   One hundred and fifty deaths occurred on
board the *Alexander*, the hulk belonging to the Messrs

Blythe. No sooner had the disease broken out in the civil prison, than it spread with great violence and rapidity through other quarters of the town. Its course was extremely eccentric, and apparently governed by no fixed law. One side of a street was sometimes assailed, while the other escaped. One house would have its dying inmates, while the next, on the same side of the street, seemed like the habitations of the Israelites, on the night of the slaughter of the first-born, to have blood sprinkled on its lintels and its door-posts, as a sign to the angel of death to pass it over. Houses situated in quarters of the town where every species of filth had been allowed to accumulate, where the air was poisoned with fetid emanations, and the inhabitants ill clad, ill fed, and predisposed to disease through vicious indulgence, escaped; while the beautiful country residence of Clairmont, situated on the breezy heights of Plaines Wilhelmes, and enjoying a delightful climate, seemed to possess peculiar attractions for the fearful disease, which swept off its possessor and several of his dependents. If the seeds of the disease were contained in the atmosphere, it was not merely in the vitiated and infected atmosphere that impended over Port Louis like dark clouds. They were contained even in that which surrounds the summits of the loftiest mountains. A Mr Gotré, panic-struck, like many of his countrymen, at the rapid spread and increasing violence of the disease, fled from Port Louis, and established himself with his family near the summit of the Pieter Both. Death, like the *atra cura* of the poet, dogged his footsteps, followed him up the lofty declivities of the Pieter Both, and seized on one of his children.   The time that elapsed between his departure from Port Louis and the appearance of cholera leaves no foundation for the supposition that he carried the germs of the disease with him from the town (were that even possible), but leads rather to the conclusion that the whole atmosphere, from the low-lying ravine in which Port Louis is situated to the loftiest summits of the Pouce and the Pieter Both, was infected.   It is a curious fact, that persons of previously sober habits, who had recourse to stimulants, under the false impression that they might serve in some sort as an antidote—and there were many such—were usually cut off; while confirmed drunkards, whose constitutions were inured to the effects of ardent spirits, and who persisted in their usual habits, in almost every case were spared.   Another analogous fact is, that of eighteen hundred Chinamen who were resident in Port Louis when cholera broke out, only two were attacked—a number bearing a very small proportion to that of those who were assailed among the other races inhabiting the island.   Are we to ascribe the escape of drunkards to the action of colonial rum upon the coatings of the stomach and the system in general, and that of Chinamen to their inordinate use of tea and opium?   Or are we to look for an explanation in the following opinion enunciated with much gravity by a medical practitioner:—" I look upon predisposition to be an impoverished or vitiated state of the blood, which acts upon the nervous system, producing depression of spirits and want of moral courage"? Is it true that drunkenness, or the excessive use of opium or tea, removes all predisposition to cholera, by preventing "an impoverished or vitiated state of the blood"? Is the blood of Chinamen and drunkards rendered, by the use of opium and rum, purer and richer than that of other men? Is the want of moral courage the result of an impoverished and vitiated state of the blood, acting upon the nervous system? If so, a bull, having richer blood than a man, would possess more moral courage; and a soldier, accused of cowardice, could plead as a valid excuse that his blood at the moment was neither very rich nor very pure. And, O Mauritians, if this original theory to account for the want of moral courage be true, in what a fearfully impoverished and vitiated state must your blood have been during the whole time of cholera!

Towards the close of May, an all but universal panic seized upon the inhabitants of Port Louis. All who could fled from the town as from a charnel-house of death. The sacred offices due to the dying and the sick were forgotten, and many literally left the dead to bury their dead. The grim phantom of death, stalking in the midst of them, froze up with his icy touch the warmth of their domestic affections, and dissolved the ties of friendship and of love. The motto of all became, as on another disastrous occasion, " Sauve qui peut." A silence that struck drearily on the heart pervaded the streets, usually thronged with sugar traders and filled with the busy hum of commerce. The doors and shutters of the houses were carefully closed, as if this precaution could exclude the entrance of the invisible but omnipresent foe. The universal silence in the centre of the town was only interrupted at times by the peal of the cathedral bells, or the hoarse chanting of the priests interceding for a departed soul, or the hollow rumbling of the carts conveying the bodies of the dead to their last home, without any of the usual pomp and pageantry of woe. It seemed to be a city of the dead, abandoned of God, and deserted by man. The only symptoms of life and movement were to be perceived in the two great outlets of the town, leading in the direction of Plaines Wilhelmes and Pamplemousses. The former leads to the Cemetery, and was usually crowded every morning during the latter part of May with vehicles of all descriptions, containing fugitives, with their most valuable effects, mixed up with donkey-carts, containing those who could no longer flee, driven by Malabars, discharging their sad office with all the stolid indifference of their race. There might be seen Æneas without Anchises—Lot leaving wife, daughters, and sons-in-law behind. Each man bore with him his *lares* and *penates*—the merchant his iron safe, the negro his bag of rice. Others, in whom the instincts of affection were stronger, carried off their parents, wives, or children, and left all else behind. The miserable blacks at the foot of the Signal Mountain, having no place of refuge in the country, shut themselves up in their huts, and sought escape from the consciousness of approaching death in the insensibility of intoxication. The Indians in Malabar Town either met death with the indifference of a fatalism which, with them, is more the result of constitution than of system, or sought to avert it by the drumming of tom-toms, or the sacrifice of goats to the goddess Kalée, the avenging Nemesis of the Hindoo faith.

The deputy-mayor and several of the town councillors fled at the first outbreak. When cholera was only spoken of as a contingency, and had not yet appeared as a dread reality, each of these men was a hero in his own eyes and in those of his constituents, pathetically eloquent about the sweetness and decorum of dying for one's country, and ready, like the late Colonel Sibthorp, to die upon the floor rather than desert his duty. But when the hour came, they chose to live and not to die, believing perhaps, with another hero of the same calibre, that discretion is the better part of valour, and that there would be little honour in dying for their country with no spectators present to report the dignity of their death. No less than five medical men succumbed in Port Louis, the victims of their devotion to the interests of their patients, and their memories are still embalmed in the grateful recollection of many who owed their lives to their unremitting care. It is a pleasing circumstance to relate, that all the ministers of the Christian religion in the colony remained faithfully on the field of duty, and that most of them were unremitting in imparting the last consolations of our holy religion to the dying. Their conduct formed a striking contrast to that of the fugitives, some of whom were professed infidels and scoffers at all religion. While the Romish priests and Protestant ministers were shewing the strength and the devotedness which faith can impart in the hour of trial, those scoffers, who professed to have no belief in God, were blanching and trembling before one of God's creatures, and hiding themselves among the remote mountains, as if, like the prophet of old, they could flee from the presence of the Lord.

The disease continued gradually to increase in violence till it reached its culminating point on the 11th of June, when 243 deaths were reported to the Civil Commissary at Port Louis. From that date there was a sensible decrease in the amount of mortality. During the four days that followed, the deaths reported were respectively 138, 168, 111, 92 ; on the 16th, the mortality suddenly rose to 213; on the 17th, it decreased to 92 ; and rose again to 129 on the 18th. From that day it diminished considerably; and on the 30th there were only seven deaths. The last case that occurred in Port Louis was in October. A Mr Ackroyd, residing in the valley between the Champ Delort and the Champ de Mars, was attacked, along with two of his children. They all died. In the month of May the population of Port Louis amounted to nearly 49,000 souls. The deaths regularly reported from the 25th of May to the 1st of August were 3492, being at the rate of about fifty *per diem*. There can be no doubt but that the mortality reached a much higher figure; but many of the Indians buried their dead by the sea-shore, and in other

solitary places, and made no declaration of the deaths
before the Civil Commissary,   It is impossible to state
with certainty the exact number of deaths caused by
cholera in 1854, throughout the whole colony, but it
was probably about fourteen thousand, or about one-
fifteenth of the whole population.

Almost as wonderful instances of the contagiousness
of cholera are related as the one mentioned by that
prince of story-tellers, Boccacio, in the introduction to
the "Decameron." He gravely informs us, that when the
plague visited Florence in 1348, the rags of a poor man
just dead were thrown into the street.   Two hogs came
up, and after rooting among the rags, and shaking them
about in their mouths, both in less than an hour turned
round and died on the spot.   The reason, perhaps, why
no hogs died a similar death in Port Louis may have
been, that all such animals found wandering on the
streets are at once conveyed to the Town-house, and sold
to the highest bidder by the mayor.   Having been kept,
therefore, in the strictest seclusion during the prevalence
of cholera, the pigs of Port Louis were preserved intact,
and thus furnished an additional argument in favour
of the general belief, that if the quarantine laws had been
strictly enforced, cholera would never have appeared.

The arrival of the *Sultany*, and the outbreak of
cholera in Port Louis, instead of being regarded as
an accidental coincidence, occupied, and still occupy,
in the public mind the relation of cause and effect.
It was currently reported and believed, that the captain of the *Sultany* was in the habit of violating the

quarantine laws, and paying visits to a woman of the name of Malfait, residing at Grand River.   This woman was a sister of the man Malfait, whose child was attacked on the 6th of May and died on the 7th.   She herself was taken ill on the 7th, and died on the 8th.   Of this story we can only say, " Se non è vero, è ben trovato." It was asserted also, that the fishermen of Grand River visited the *Sultany,* and exchanged their fish for rice. A Mr Berichon declared that he saw every evening a fisherman's boat, bearing the name of *Mouton,* communicate with the *Sultany* while she was in quarantine. An advocate of the name of Savy was said to be acquainted with a case of communication with the *Sultany.*   Examined upon the subject, Savy answered with the laconic indistinctness of a man who does not wish to compromise himself, " That after having consulted with his friends, he could not disclose the facts that occurred at his office with regard to the fact of communication with the *Sultany.*"   The report was, that Savy, one of a class of legal practitioners peculiar to Mauritius, had assisted the captain of the *Sultany* in recovering a box of sovereigns which he had entrusted to the keeping of the woman Malfait, and which her relations were unwilling to give up.   Savy's ambiguous answer tended to confirm this report.

All the medical men examined, with the exception of two, expressed their belief that cholera was infectious, and might be communicated by intercourse between man and man.   The instances adduced are favourable to this theory, and, in fact, can scarcely be explained on any other, unless we are to suppose that these men were guilty of a breach of good faith, or that they saw the facts of the case through such a distorted medium of prejudice as to render their evidence valueless. If we admit that the instances about to be cited are literally true, the conclusion that cholera is in certain cases communicable by human intercourse, seems unavoidable. It is affirmed, in general terms, that, in the country districts, in nine cases out of ten, the first victims had had intercourse with persons labouring under the disease, either by touch or by breathing the same air. At the Rivière de Rempart, according to Dr Gouly, it was a Creole woman who first introduced the disease. At Flacq, according to Dr Grivot, it was a child just arrived from Port Louis. At Grand Port, it was a coachman who had driven some person from Port Louis. At the Savanne, it was a young girl who left Port Louis on the 28th of May, and was attacked on the 29th. On the 1st of June, cholera broke out throughout the whole district. At Plaines Wilhelmes, the disease was introduced by those who had fled from Port Louis, and it appears to have been the same in all the country districts. Country cousins—a class not usually very popular among the denizens of towns—were never so much in demand as during the prevalence of cholera. Wherever a distant relationship could be traced, the houses of the poor *habitans* were crowded with fugitives from Port Louis. One small house at Black River, containing only one small bed-room, afforded shelter to sixteen persons, of different sexes, for upwards of a month, and, singular to relate, they all escaped. In many cases, the outbreak of cholera was owing mainly or wholly to the influence of fear. The fugitives, with their imaginations excited by the horrors which they had witnessed at Port Louis, gave such harrowing details of the ravages of the fearful scourge, that many, on listening to them, were seized at once with all the preliminary symptoms, and in many cases cut off. A singular instance of this occurred within the experience of the writer of these pages. A female servant, a Creole, in his employment, was residing with his family in one of the country districts near Port Louis about the beginning of June. She received a visit one day from her father, a carpenter belonging to Port Louis. His imagination had been strongly excited by the number of funerals which he had witnessed in passing through Moka Street, and he had had recourse to colonial rum as a means of warding off his terrors. The girl was perfectly well at nine o'clock in the evening, though rather frightened by the stories related by her father. The next morning she did not appear at the usual hour. On an entrance into the cottage which she occupied being effected, she and her father were found both stretched on the floor, with their limbs contorted with the horrible cramp which marks one of the last stages of cholera. The father was speechless and dying, and the poor girl could only look up with an expression of agony and terror that can never be forgotten, and feebly mutter, " Frottez." No medical man could be obtained. She was placed in a carriage in order to be conveyed to the hospital. The coachman, panic-struck, overturned the carriage at a few hundred yards from the house, and she was precipitated into the road. This accident produced a momentary reaction, and, for a time, when conveyed to town and subjected to proper medical treatment, she gave fair hopes of recovery. This hope, however, was not realised. She soon followed her father to the grave. This incident would, no doubt, be regarded by the contagionists as favourable to their theory; but the attack seems rather to have been the result of excessive fear, excited by the detail of the ravages committed by the pestilence in Port Louis. The mind exercises a powerful influence in such cases, and the best preventive against cholera is a calm, self-possessed spirit, in *utrumque paratus.* There are other cases, however, reported by respectable medical men, where the conclusion that cholera is in certain cases contagious seems inevitable. A few of these may be mentioned. A Mr Dubois was attacked with cholera. His servant remained with him, and spent two days and a night in rubbing him. After his death, the servant himself was attacked with cholera. His wife waited upon him, and died on the second day; and his mother-in-law, who did not live in the same house, having come to wait upon them during their illness, was herself attacked, and speedily succumbed. On the property Hochet, upon the road to Long Mountain, there were no cases of cholera for several days. They were in the habit of sending to town daily for such provisions as they required. A man on his return from town was seized with cholera, and on this small property, occupied by about twenty persons, fifteen died in succession. The coachman of Mr D'Epinay, named Frank, an Englishman, on his arrival from town, found his child ill; he remained to nurse it, and after witnessing the death of his wife and his three children, he himself was attacked, and died after a day's illness. It is worthy of remark, that everything on this establishment was in a state of perfect cleanliness, and that no cases of cholera occurred in the neighbouring houses, where there had been no communication with the town. A young girl went to count the funerals in Moka Street, which leads to the Cemetery; on her return, she was seized with cholera. The whole population of that street were attacked, one after another, and scarcely one escaped. There was constant communication between the inhabitants of the different houses, who, as often happens in Port Louis, were all more or less related to each other. There are several brothers at Port Louis of the name of Pitchen, all living with their families in different streets of the town. One of the brothers was attacked. The different families came to visit him. Some days after there were in every one of these families, and in their different houses, persons attacked with cholera. These cases are extracted from the report of Dr Colin, an intelligent young physician of Port Louis, whose good faith is beyond all suspicion. A Dr Perrot, residing at Plaines Wilhelmes, declares that he did not meet with a single case of cholera where communication with infected places could not be traced, and states as a singular fact, that cholera manifested itself at Plaines Wilhelmes only when the wind was blowing from the town in the direction of that quarter, and especially in the houses of persons who had been in Port Louis. Numerous facts of the same character, all tending to establish the contagiousness of cholera, might be quoted from the reports of the other medical men in Mauritius, all of whom, with the exception of two, are contagionists; but, as they do not present any new or interesting features, it is unnecessary to dwell upon them.

In November, cholera broke out at Flacq. The circumstances connected with its appearance in that district are curious, and seem to prove beyond a doubt what few in Mauritius would now deny—that cholera is infectious, and that places infected may retain the seeds of infection for a considerable period after the disease has disappeared from the locality. On the property Clemencia, at Flacq, there was a shop, where two persons had died during the time of the first epidemic. Since that time the shop had remained shut. On the 13th of November, a woman of the name of Alfred, the sister-in-law of the proprietor of the shop, took it into her head to look whether a shawl which she had left in the shop was still there. She caused a shutter to be opened, and put only her head inside. She was repelled by the offensive odour exhaled from the room, and immediately withdrew. The same night she was taken ill, and next day she died. Her adopted child, two years of age, was attacked the same day, and died after an illness of twenty-four hours. From her house the epidemic spread in a gradually increasing circle, and no less than seventy-eight cases of cholera presented themselves, after it had ceased for more than three months in every other district of the island, with the exception of the solitary case of the family Ackroyd.

It might have been expected that the Mauritians, smarting under the remembrance of this severe visitation, and anxious to avoid its recurrence, would have proceeded to cover their open drains, to clean their streets, to ventilate their houses, and to adopt those other sanitary measures which tend to check, if not to avert the ravages of cholera. The Town Council and the press were too busily engaged in delivering philippics against the local Government to occupy themselves with such insignificant matters. The system of *laissez aller* is so innate to the Creole character, that all the lessons of their recent sad experience were speedily forgotten, and they looked to the strict enforcement of the quarantine laws as the only condition necessary to the enjoyment of perfect immunity from another outbreak of cholera. Matters continued in this state of false security till the month of January 1856, when two vessels, the *Hyderee* and *Futteh Mobarruck*, arrived at Port Louis, with a cargo of Coolie labourers. Neither of these vessels had a clean bill of health, and the rumour spread rapidly through the town that

cholera was on board.   There is no evidence that such
was the case at the moment of their arrival.   It may
be easily conceived, that when several hundred Indians
are crowded into a ship, with no other doctor on board
than that greatest of all charlatans, a native practitioner,
and without sufficient provision for the enforcement of
cleanliness, or the cooking of their rice, which, during
a gale, they are sometimes obliged to eat raw or to
starve, cases of dysentery and severe diarrhœa will
occur.   When the patients are landed at once, and
subjected to proper treatment, these diseases speedily
disappear, and the Coolie is restored to his former
vigour.   Unfortunately for the poor Coolies on board
these ships, Port Louis was seized with a cholera panic,
a species of insanity that may now be regarded as
endemic.   The Government, yielding to the popular
clamour and the threats of the press, ordered the 656
Coolies to be disembarked on Flat and Gabriel Islands,
two miserable rocks, a few miles from Port Louis,
where no sufficient provision had been made for affording them shelter and food.   The condition of these
miserable wretches was truly deplorable.   The quarantine laws, strictly enforced, forbade them to land—the
open sea and the bare rocks offered them only a grave.
In the course of a short time the bones of two hundred
Coolies were bleaching on these barren rocks, the victims
of Creole cowardice and Government mismanagement.
This fearful mortality created little sensation among the
Creoles.   Cholera had broken out in Port Louis, and
they had no sympathy for any suffering save their

own.   The mortality, though considerable, was not so great as in 1854.   In the case of any public disaster the Creoles must always have a victim, and on this occasion they selected the Governor.   He was represented as gloating over the sufferings of his subjects, like the Roman Emperor of old, and indulging in every kind of festivity, while Port Louis was clad in sackcloth and ashes.*   Comparisons were drawn between his conduct, in shutting himself up at Reduit, and that of the Governor of Malta, who during the prevalence of cholera visited the public hospitals, and did every thing in his power to relieve the suffering, and to arrest the progress of the malady.   The Genius of cholera was introduced, and represented as writing upon the wall of the Governor's banqueting hall its "Mene, Tekel," like the fingers of a man's hand at Belshazzar's feast. The guardian angel of Mauritius covered her face, and wept over her slaughtered children in the "leaders" of the local press ; but there was neither man nor angel to lament the miserable Coolies, perishing by scores on Flat and Gabriel Islands.   While cholera still existed in Port Louis, though its ravages were less intense, another Coolie ship, the *Shah Jehan*, arrived in the harbour.   Next morning the corners of the principal streets and thoroughfares were covered with placards, announcing that there was cholera on board the *Shah Jehan*, and calling upon the people to assemble at Government House.   Excited groups might be seen

* It is almost needless to say that there was no truth in these charges.

reading these placards with pale faces, or discussing with violent gesticulations the propriety of some public demonstration against the Government. Though the placards were spread over the whole town, such was the remissness of the police and civil authorities that no measures were adopted for the protection of Government House, which was invaded towards noon by a mob, which demanded to see the Governor. Several orators mounted temporary rostrums, and delivered exciting addresses, calling upon their hearers, if their wives and children were dear to them, to insist upon the *Shah Jehan* being sent off to sea again. The Governor appeared upon the balcony, but his presence only increased the uproar. In a moment of inadvertence, he happened to turn his back upon the assembly, and the dignity of King Mob was very much hurt in consequence. An amusing illustration of the Creole character may be found in the fact, that when the Governor's conduct was criticised afterwards by the press, much more blame was attached to his having turned his back upon the mob, than to his having allowed the *Shah Jehan* to enter the harbour. It was proposed that the guns of the citadel should be turned against the offending vessel, and the Governor, yielding to the popular clamour, was induced to order her into quarantine. The ravages of cholera among the Coolies on board, who were worn out by the sea voyage, and destitute of all the care and attention which their case required, were very great. Mauritius, however, is so isolated, and so little within the reach of public opinion at home, that these cases, bad as they were, might have led to no amelioration of the sanitary arrangements connected with the reception of Coolies arriving in the colony, had there not been on the spot an Indian official interested in the welfare of the Coolies, who, on his return to India, reported the case to the Government.   The following article appeared in the *Friend of India* of the 7th of August 1856 :—

"We recently warned all Indian readers, in search of health or anxious for leisure, to avoid a visit to the Mauritius.   Port Louis, it is true, is easy of access.   It is within the Indian limits, to the great attraction of all who adhere to the old rules of military leave.   The island itself is beautiful enough to allure even those who have seen Sicily, and the planters are said to be hospitable in the extreme, but the curse of ignorance is over all.   The islanders are determined, in spite of all medical evidence and all experiments of every Indian visitor, and everybody else with a brain, to believe that cholera is contagious.   The unhappy traveller, therefore, is subjected to all the horrors of a worse than Russian quarantine.   If a Coolie or Lascar on board has an attack of diarrhœa, if a man of the crew becomes delirious with drink, it is all over with the voyager.   The island goes mad.   Port Louis is in an uproar.   The Municipality pass treasonable resolutions. The mob surrounds the Governor's house.   The unlucky officials, suspected because they are possessed of brains, are spurred and harassed into injustice, and the unhappy vessel is placed for weeks in a quarantine, which too often produces the evil the islanders are striving to avoid. If this were all, we should confine ourselves to a warning to intending tourists. It is doubtless disagreeable and even dangerous to be detained for weeks on a barren rock, fed with unwholesome food, and drenched with fetid water. Those Europeans, however, who proceed there, knowing these facts, have only themselves to blame, and are probably compelled by reasons which justify them in braving even Mauritius hospitality. The case is different as regards the Coolies. They are sent thither under official protection, under an implied guarantee that their lives shall not be sacrified to the ignorant selfishness of a Creole mob. We are assured in the most positive manner, that under existing regulations they are sacrificed—we had almost written murdered—in scores at a time. In January of this year, the *Hyderee* and *Futteh Mobarruck* arrived in Port Louis with a cargo of Coolies. There were a few cases of severe diarrhœa on board, such as will occur among all large assemblages of natives. They were not, however, cases of cholera. The rumour, however, was sufficient. Port Louis displayed the usual symptoms of incipient insanity, and the vessels were ordered off to Flat or Gabriel Islands. These are two rocks in the midst of the sea, about ten miles from the town. The Coolies, 656 in number, worn out with sea-sickness, want of exercise, and all the *désagrémens* incidental to a sea voyage, were turned out upon the islets. Nothing was given them for shelter, no wood, no leaves, no grass, not even mud for building huts. The food was insufficient, the water was fetid, the exposure was such as even natives are unable to endure, Cholera, fever, and acute dysentery were raging among them all at once, and, as we are positively assured, two hundred men perished on the rock.

"At the same time cholera broke out in Port Louis. The contagion had, of course, spread from Gabriel Island, but as this is ten miles off, and there had been no communication, the wiseacres seemed almost puzzled. At last it was discovered that the steamer *Victoria* had carried provisions there, that one man had landed, and that this man had died of cholera. What more was required? True, the man had been suffering for weeks. True, the body had been thrown into the sea, miles away from Port Louis, and none of the people on board caught the disease. No evidence, however clear, weighs with fanatics; the islanders were confirmed in their belief, and the deaths of the unfortunate Bengalees were condoned. This, however, is not all. Men are always cruel when inspired by selfishness and fear; but the Mauritians went a step further. The cholera was raging in the island when the *Shah Jehan* arrived. Even if the disease had been raging on board, and if the theory of contagion had been as true as it is absurd, there was no reason for delay. The disease could not be increased by the poor Coolies. There was no proof apparently that the cholera was on board, and the immigrants ran far more risk than their inhospitable

employers.   No matter they were natives imported
under every assurance of kindness and protection.
Port Louis rose.   The Governor was coerced into an
order sending the vessel into quarantine, and there it
remained till weeks had become months.   Cholera of
course broke out.   The Coolies died in scores, while
the Creoles raved on about the danger of contagion,
and refused to make the most ordinary efforts for sanitary reform.   The Municipality sits and accuses the
Governor ; the planters sit and lecture the Governor ;
the people gesticulate and threaten the Governor ; and,
meanwhile, in that town of close streets, there is not
one water-closet or one covered drain.   The matter de-
serves, and will, we hope, receive the most serious attention of the Government of India.   The follies of the
Mauritians are nothing to any of us.   They may believe
they are hospitable, or that the sun goes round the
earth, or that Port Louis is an enlightened city, or any
other absurdity they please.   But even ignorance and
credulity are not excuses for the wholesale sacrifice of
our fellow-subjects.   This particular folly affects the
character for good faith of the Government of India.
The Coolies are attracted to the Mauritius by an official
pledge that their engagements shall be kept ; that they
shall be fairly treated and protected in the enjoyment
of their rights.   That pledge has been broken in a
manner as silly as inhuman, and it is to the Government of India alone that the survivors look for redress.
The remedy is in its own hands.   Without these
Coolies, whom they thus leave to die, the Mauritians

would be the happy possessors of a barren rock.   We cannot appeal to their humanity, but we may to their thirst for dollars.   Let the Government suspend the law permitting Coolies to be despatched to the Mauritius, until the planters have invented some reasonable system which shall. at least ensure to its subjects some decent food, water not too brackish to drink, and some covering, if it be only as much as we should give to bullocks.   Six months' suspension would probably teach the Creoles, that even if quarantine be enforced to conciliate their prejudices, it need not necessarily involve a massacre."

The indignation excited by this article in Mauritius may be easily conceived.   The planters, instead of trying to disprove the facts which it contained, or to remedy the evil to which it pointed, indulged in scurrilous abuse of the writer, and imputed to him every motive save the true one—a desire to see justice done, and the good faith of the Government of India vindicated.   The Governor of Mauritius might be coerced by the clamour of a Creole mob; the Government of India was beyond their reach.   The Supreme Council passed an ordinance suspending the importation of Coolie emigrants to Mauritius until the quarantine regulations should be placed on a more satisfactory footing, and accommodation provided for those who, from having a foul bill of health, might be prevented from landing.   The arrival of this intelligence in a colony which owes all its prosperity to Coolie labour, caused nearly as great a panic as the dread of cholera.

The Chamber of Agriculture proposed to send one of its members to Calcutta to intercede with the Government of India, but this proposal was never carried into effect. With such glaring facts against them, the astutest of their number would have found it rather difficult to make the worse appear the better cause. The temporary suspension of Coolie emigration has now been removed. Accommodation of such a nature as to prevent the possibility of the recurrence of similar disasters, has been provided for immigrants placed in temporary quarantine; but no regulations, however strictly enforced, will ever be sufficient to ward off cholera from this colony. If the planters *will* have Coolies from India, they must be prepared to incur the risk of cholera; if they *will* escape that risk, they must be prepared to make sugar without Coolie labour. It is a question of the relative value of life and sugar, and one of the two alternatives seems inevitable. But, in truth, they have less to dread from the Coolies imported from India, than from the Creoles and Coolies crowded together in the narrow streets and festering lanes of Port Louis, in houses that are ill ventilated, and filled with the miasma of the reeking drains in their neighbourhood. It has become the fashion of late years to ascribe all the disease in the colony to the influx of Coolie immigrants; and no doubt every addition to the population, from whatever quarter, must tend to increase the generating causes of disease, so long as the present population is crowded together in houses that were barely sufficient for the accommodation of the inhabitants ten years ago. The erection of well-ventilated houses, furnished with the conveniences of civilised life, the use of healthy and nutritive food, cleanliness of person, the suppression of the sale of "poison" under the name of arrack, and the covering of the open drains, will do more to ward off cholera than all the quarantine regulations that the ingenuity or the terror of man can ever devise.

After cholera, the disease which has committed the greatest ravages in the colony is small-pox. The Creoles have a traditionary dread of this malady, owing to the population having been decimated by an outbreak which occasioned a fearful mortality among the slaves in 1782. Vaccination was entirely neglected, until the Government lately directed their attention to the subject, and appointed an officer to perform the operation on the poorer classes gratuitously. There is still a strong prejudice against it among the blacks; and when the colony was visited with this disease in 1856, they were the greatest sufferers.

While this colony is exempt from the yellow fever of the West Indian islands, there is a species of typhoid fever which prevails more or less throughout the whole year, in those quarters of Port Louis that are inhabited by the lower classes. It is supposed to be of Indian origin, and is usually known as the Bombay fever. It is said to have been unknown till the introduction of the Coolie immigrants; but its origin ought to be referred to local causes—to an overcrowded population, residing in unhealthy localities, and breathing a polluted atmosphere, and to the improper nature of the food used by a large portion of the inhabitants. I have not met with a single case of Bombay fever among the English residents who live in the country or the better parts of the town; but the mortality caused by it among the Creoles and the Coolies at certain seasons is very great. Owing to the nature of the food and the deteriorating influences of a tropical climate, they have not the same stamina as the English, and succumb beneath diseases from which the latter generally escape.

The most fearful and loathsome of all the diseases prevalent among the Creoles is *leprosy.* Its origin is ascribed to different causes—to the constant intermarriage of the same families, to the excessive use of lard in cooking, and to the influence of climate. The taint of leprosy is as much dreaded as the taint of colour. The families subject to this disease are known, and intermarriage with them carefully avoided. A hospital has been provided in one of the dependencies of Mauritius for the reception of those labouring under the more violent forms of the disease.

Consumption is of frequent occurrence, especially among the Coolies. Their exposure in the open air, without sufficient clothing, and the difference between the temperature of India and that of Mauritius, may have some influence in producing this effect. No one acquainted with Mauritius could ever place it on the same footing as Madeira, or recommend it as a sanatarium for those labouring under pulmonary complaints. Some years ago, thirty soldiers, belonging to other regiments, and labouring under consumption, were drafted into a regiment under orders for Mauritius. This was done under the erroneous impression that the climate of Mauritius was favourable to the recovery of consumptive patients. All of these men died within a comparatively short period after their arrival. Those also who have a hereditary tendency to gout, would do well to avoid a permanent residence in this colony. Paralytic disorders and severe rheumatism are also common.

Dysentery and liver complaint are the two diseases most fatal to the British soldiers. The reckless use of the arrack sold in the public canteens predisposes them to these diseases; and yet, from the War Office returns, it appears that the mortality among the soldiers stationed here is not so great as in other parts of the world, usually esteemed more healthy. Temperance, sea-bathing, and an umbrella are the best preventives against these diseases. Old residenters believe the use of pure water to be highly dangerous, and almost certain to superinduce dysentery. Claret and water is thought to be the safest beverage. The prejudice against water appears to have been handed down from the days of the early colonists, who relate that it gave the cramp to young ducks, and the bloody flux to those who drank it. It is to be observed, however, that this effect was only produced by water shaded by wood from the influence of the sun, while the prejudice of the old residenters extends to water of all kinds, whether shaded by the sun or otherwise.

The climate of Mauritius has either deteriorated of late years, or has been represented in too favourable a light by former travellers. The island has been described as a little paradise, enjoying a delicious climate, and immunity from all those diseases that are peculiar to the tropics. Those, however, who have lived in it for years have been led to form a different opinion. If drunken, dishonest servants, extravagant charges for inferior articles, scurrilous attacks on private character by a licentious press, the consciousness of being cheated at all hands without any means of redress, and the enervating influences of a climate that soon wears out the strongest constitution and the most vigorous mind, constitute a paradise, Mauritius has undoubted claims to that character. There is no disease peculiar to the tropics that may not be found there, with the single exception of yellow fever. The wearing influences of the climate arise, not only from the almost insupportable heat of the sun during two-thirds of the year, but also from the softness of the air, which deprives the body of all strength, and the mind of all elasticity, and superinduces a general listlessness and impassibility of character, which never fail to strike a stranger on his first arrival. Life is so monotonous, so destitute of all exciting impressions and animating sensations, so unmarked by any of those events that, in other countries, tend to divert the thoughts, and to prevent the mind from morbidly preying upon itself, that many sink into a half-unconscious state of existence, often more destructive to health than an attack of disease. Day after day, the bright burning sun rises at the same hour, pursues the same course, and sinks into the same place of rest. The eternal sunshine becomes tiresome, and the European, at least, longs for the climate of Europe, with its varying seasons and its agreeable changes. The island is so limited in extent, that one has the feeling of being compressed within too narrow space, and longs for those vast continents where the mind can expatiate, without being hemmed in by the ocean, and where one can travel for successive weeks, without arriving at what appears to be the end of the world. Life in the Mauritius resembles, in a great measure, solitary imprisonment in a stifling atmosphere, and produces much the same effect upon the mind and the body. Those who become once habituated to it may extend their dreary monotonous lives to the usual span of mortal existence, but many die of mere mental inanition, or have recourse to dissipation, as a means of temporary escape from that *ennui* that weighs upon their spirits. The slaves seem to have participated largely in this feeling, and to have had recourse to strange means in order to escape from it. They often fled to the mountains, in order to escape from the monotonous life of the plantation. Sometimes they committed crimes entailing capital punishment, from the same motive, deeming death itself preferable to the life which they led. Cases of suicide, arising from the same cause, were not uncommon ; and I have known instances of soldiers committing breaches of military discipline, for which they could assign no motive, save the desire to vary, even by punishment, the otherwise dull tenor of their monotonous existence.   The only effective cure for this disease is change of scenery; and none who wish to enjoy the greatest of all earthly blessings, the *mens sana in corpore sano,* should remain in Mauritius more than five years at a time.   The monotony of a voyage of three months at sea, is lively when compared with the gayest season in the island of canes and hurricanes.

CHAPTER V.

THE productive power of Mauritius was not known till
after the abolition of slavery. Whatever effect that
measure may have produced in other colonies, in Mauritius it cannot be regarded as otherwise than a positive
benefit. It introduced a new system of culture, and a
new class of labourers. The quantity of sugar exported
from Mauritius at the present day, when compared with
that produced before the emancipation of the slaves,
affords the most convincing proof that free labour,
when attainable, is far more productive than slave
labour. In 1835, the quantity of sugar exported from
Mauritius, amounted to 648,545 quintals (100 lbs.
French). In 1845, it amounted to 963,000 quintals.
M'Culloch stated some years before that it had reached
the acme of production, and it is said that Mr Huskisson
predicted that the produce of the colony could never ex-

ceed 8000 tons of sugar. If Mr Huskisson were alive at the present day, he would be astonished to learn that 113,595 tons of sugar, or more than fourteen times the quantity which he regarded as the maximum of Mauritius produce, was exported from the colony in 1856. This increase in the produce of the colony has been owing exclusively to the introduction of Coolie labourers from India. No doubt a larger amount of capital has been embarked in the cultivation of the soil, and improved machinery has been introduced from England and France, but that has been the consequence of the facility of obtaining Indian labour, the primary cause of the island's prosperity at the present day. If Mauritius, instead of being situated in the Indian Ocean, within a few weeks' sailing of the great Indian peninsula, teeming with inhabitants, had occupied the same latitude as the West Indian Islands, instead of having quadrupled the quantity of sugar produced within a few years back, it would now have been sunk in the same ruinous condition as these unfortunate dependencies of the British crown. The abolition of slavery would have been its death-blow, and instead of having its sloping plains and central high lands covered with the rustling cane, and the natural beauty of its scenery diversified by bands of busy labourers, and the smoke of working *usines*, the whole island might soon have relapsed into its original state, and if not abandoned, as at a former period by the Dutch, retained only by the British for the conveniences which its harbour affords to their Indian shipping. Its nearness to the Indian peninsula, and the facility of procuring Indian labour, saved it from this fate.

It is unnecessary to dwell upon the effects which the emancipation of the slaves produced upon the labour market. These effects were the same as in the West Indian Islands, with this difference that the emancipated slaves having been formerly treated with greater harshness than those in the West Indies, by their French masters, were, on that account, the more averse to labouring in their fields. They preferred a life of indolent ease, or occupied themselves in cultivating small patches of land, which, owing to the kindliness of the soil, were sufficient for their subsistence. If they did labour at times on the cane-fields, it was only to procure a little money to satisfy their wants, or to gratify their vanity. When their object was attained, they returned to that state of indolent, ambitionless existence, which seems to be the normal condition of the African race.

To escape from this unenviable position, the planters, with the assistance and sanction of the local Government, had recourse to the Indian peninsula. In the interior of India, there are millions of natives condemned to constant toil, and receiving for their labour the lowest remuneration necessary for subsistence. Acquainted with the value of money, and ambitious to amass sufficient wealth to raise them to the envied position of land-proprietors in their native villages—possessed of bone and muscle, fitting them for the most arduous labour—and anxious to obtain a higher remuneration than the native labour market offered, the hill Coolies of India were as ready to embark, as the planters of Mauritius to welcome them to their shores.

To prevent injustice and disorder, the local Government, instead of allowing the planters to supply themselves with labourers from India without control, wisely took the matter in hand, and introduced salutary arrangements regulating the introduction of Coolie immigrants. If the labour market in India had been left open to free trade, and the planters of Mauritius been allowed to introduce as many labourers as they chose, the result would have been that the island would have been crowded with Coolies. From the surplus of labour in the market, these men would have been obliged to labour at a low rate of wages, in a colony where all the necessaries of life are extremely dear. Without the protection of Government also, there would have been a danger of these men being treated with injustice, and reduced even to a state of absolute slavery, when employed by unprincipled masters.

To prevent the island from being overcrowded with Coolies, the Government took care that the annual importation should be regulated according to the real wants of the colony. An estimate was made beforehand of the number of Coolies that would be required for the ensuing year, and care taken that the labourers introduced should not exceed that number. To prevent anything like a system of kidnapping (such as is largely practised in the neighbouring island of Bourbon)*

* The Coolies of India being now on their guard, the authorities of Bourbon have had recoursé to the Kingsmills' Islands to supply the deficiency in the labour market.

from springing up, Government agents were appointed in the chief towns of the three Indian Presidencies. These agents explain to intending emigrants the terms of their engagement, procure ships for their conveyance, and superintend their embarkation. The number of the Indians embarked is proportioned to the tonnage of the vessel. Two children count for one full-grown man. When the stranger reads that the *Ackbar* has arrived at Mauritius with $277\frac{1}{2}$ Coolies, he must not imagine that any unfortunate Goolab or Ramosamy has left the half of his body behind him. There is an odd child on board, that is all.

The comfort of the Coolies on board ship depends very much on the kindness and conscientiousness of the captain, in attending to their comforts, and taking care that the part of the ship occupied by them is kept clean and well ventilated. Government should make it imperative that a properly qualified medical man should accompany every cargo of Coolies. It is a mere mockery to secure the services of a native practitioner. When three hundred Coolies are crowded on board a ship, from their habits, diseases will naturally spring up among them ; and if there be no medical man on board, there must be a frequent and heavy sacrifice of human life. Diseases that might be easily checked at first, prove fatal through neglect. Cases of cholera will at times occur. A medical man may not be able to cure these cases, but he may do much in arresting the progress of the disease among the others, and in preventing that panic the spread of which kills more than the disease itself.

When the Coolie vessel arrives at the Mauritius, and shews a satisfactory bill of health, the Government protector, or his representative, goes on board, and conducts the immigrants to the Bagne, a large building situated near the shore, and used as a depôt for their reception. If the vessel cannot shew a clean bill of health, or if a cholera panic be prevalent at Port Louis, the Coolies are placed in quarantine. The horrors of such a position are described in another part of this work. It is but justice, however, to mention, that since the suspension of Coolie emigration by the Indian Government in 1856, the accommodation for the Coolies placed in temporary quarantine has been very much improved, so as to prevent a repetition of the dreadful scenes exhibited on Flat and Gabriel Islands during the previous part of the same year. It is not a pleasant sight to witness the disembarkation of some three hundred Coolies after a voyage of three weeks. They have not been able on board ship to perform their usual ablutions, or to wash their scanty supply of clothing. They have all been labouring more or less under sea-sickness, and have not been able to have their food properly cooked at sea. The spectator cannot fail to be struck with their miserable, squalid, emaciated appearance, and their general resemblance, save in the matter of complexion and clothing, to those wretched beings whom the Irish steamers land on the wharfs of Liverpool and Glasgow. There is in their appearance an air of general helplessness, such as shews the wisdom of the Government in watching over their interests. The Mauritius planters

often point with much complacency to the contrast between the miserable specimens of humanity landed on
their shores from India, and the plump, healthy, muscular men embarking for the same country at the end
of three years, as a proof of the excellent treatment
which the latter have received at their hands during the
period of their engagement. This contrast can scarcely
be regarded as a fair test of the improvement effected
in the Coolie's physical condition during his residence
in Mauritius. A Frenchman landing at Folkestone,
after crossing the Channel, is not a fair specimen of his
race. An Englishman would scarcely be justified in
judging of the improving effect which a few weeks' residence in England has produced on his French neighbour, by the contrast between the seedy, sickly, unwholesome appearance which he presents at Folkestone,
and the jaunty, spruce, self-satisfied air with which he
steps on board the steamer to return to his own country. When he lands at Boulogne, he looks much the
same man as when he landed at Folkestone, equally an
object of commiseration, from his utterly woe-begone
appearance. It is the same with the Indian when he
returns to his native shores; he looks to the full as
squalid and miserable as when he landed in Mauritius.
We refer merely to his personal appearance, and to the
insufficiency of the contrast between his appearance at
landing and re-embarking, as a test to judge of the
physical effect produced upon him by his residence in
the colony. There can be no doubt but that mentally
he is a different man. His intellect has been sharpened,

and his mind divested of many foolish prejudices, through intercourse with others, and the dissolution of those ties which, in his native land, fettered all freedom of thought, and made him a mere working machine. The greatest advantage, however, which he has reaped, is the feeling of self-respect. He has worked like a man, and earned a fair return for his labour. He feels that he occupies a place in the social system, and lays aside, in his intercourse with Europeans, those cringing, fawning, servile manners, so characteristic of his countrymen in India.

The immigrants are conducted to the depôt, where they remain two days, during which they are instructed in reference to the labour they have to perform, and the wages to which they are entitled. If there happens to be a scarcity of labourers at the moment, or if the sugar crop is nearly ready, the Bagne is surrounded during these two days with eager planters, anxious to secure for themselves the newly-arrived immigrants, and not over-scrupulous about the means they employ to gain this end. As the Coolie is ignorant of French, and the French planter equally ignorant of the different languages of India, intercourse between them is conducted through the medium of a class of natives known as *sirdars*. The services of one of these men are secured by the planter, just in the same way as the services of a barrister are secured by his client. A retaining fee is paid, and the eloquence of the *sirdar* is employed in his behalf. The scene presented in the large room of the Bagne during these two days affords a

subject worthy of the pencil of Hogarth.   It is filled
with Coolies.   Some of them are standing in groups,
and listening to the praises bestowed by the *sirdars* on
their employers.   Of course, they are represented as
approaching almost to perfection, and their plantations
described as a sort of paradises.   If they engage with
them, they will receive the highest wages for the smallest amount of labour.   If they engage with any one
else, they will have short rations, and their wages *cut
down* to the half of the amount promised.   Others of
the Coolies are prostrate on the floor, as yet too imperfectly recovered from sea-sickness to listen to the eloquence of the *sirdars,* or to care much what may be
their future fate.   In the background may be seen the
planters, hardy, bronzed, bearded men, watching the
effect of the *sirdars'* eloquence upon their hearers, and
imperfectly concealing their anxiety about the result.

The *sirdars* are not the only class employed to engage the Coolie labourers.   There are other parties connected with the Bagne, who, from having acquired the
native languages, have considerable influence among
them.   One of these, a clerk with a salary of £7 a
month, is said to have managed matters so well, that
at the end of a few years he was enabled to retire with
a comfortable little independence of about £12,000,
received from the planters and others, for services rendered.   Loose as the system of government at Mauritius is, the corruption that had crept into this depart-
ment became at length so glaring, that the matter was
reported to the Home Government.   Whether the mea-

sures adopted in consequence will check the abuse
alluded to, remains to be seen.

The Coolies are engaged for a period of three years.
Several abortive attempts have been made of late years
to have the period of their engagement extended to five
years. The Home Government have most wisely refused to accede to this proposal. If they had done so,
the system of Coolie immigration would soon have de-
generated into a species of slavery. Even under the
present arrangement it requires the strictest vigilance
on the part of the local authorities to enforce the terms
of the engagement. These are, that for a period of three
years the Coolie shall receive wages amounting to seven
rupees per month, with fifty pounds of rice, four pounds
of dholl—a kind of pulse—four pounds of salt fish, and
one pound of salt, as rations. If these terms were
strictly observed, the condition of the Coolie in Mauritius would be enviable, when compared with that which
he occupied in his own country. If his employer is an
honest man, and pays him his wages regularly, he has
no difficulty in saving three or four rupees a-month,
which he can place in the savings' bank, where he will
receive five per cent. interest for it. Many of the
Coolies, having no faith in this institution, prefer to
bury their money in the ground, where it is sometimes
discovered and carried off by their companions. Much
of the silver coin circulating in the colony is of a dingy
dark colour, in consequence of having been buried in
the ground by the Coolies. There can be no doubt but
that, under the present system, with all the vigilance

that the local authorities employ, there are frequent cases of injustice in the treatment of the Coolies. If a labourer happens to be one day absent from his work, his employer is entitled to exact two days' labour in return, or to cut off the price of two days' labour from his monthly wages. It might be easily shewn that this power is liable to gross abuse when exercised by an un-principled employer, whose interest it may be at times to provoke his labourers to desert his service. When he does not require the labour of all his Coolies, which happens at certain seasons, he may treat some of them in such a way as to lead them to desert, and thus he gains a double advantage—he escapes from the neces-sity of nourishing them during their absence, and is entitled to cut off two days' wages for every day they have been absent when they return. The system of cutting the wages *(couper les gages)* is not confined to mere absence. It extends to all possible offences, real or imaginary, and when it is practised by a master in-genious in discovering faults, the poor labourer, at the end of the month, often finds himself mulcted of a large portion of his hard-won earnings. His only mode of redress is to summon his master before the local magistrate, where, in consequence of his ignorance of French, he is placed at a great disadvantage, and except in very glaring cases, rarely obtains justice.

The Coolie huts on the sugar estates are usually in the form of a square, built of mud, and thatched with grass. Formerly little attention was paid to the enforcement of cleanliness in their camps ; but since the great mortality

occasioned by cholera in 1854, more attention has been
paid to this subject, though there is still much room
for improvement.   A medical man receives a certain
sum every year to visit the different estates, and those
labouring under complaints requiring constant care are
admitted into the Civil Hospital in Port Louis.   There
is a strong antipathy against this institution among the
Creole and Coolie population, and few avail themselves
of the advantages which it offers unless they are compelled by necessity.

Whether Mauritius be favourable or otherwise in
point of health to the Coolie population, is a question
which in the absence of the necessary data cannot be
solved.   The large mortality among that class in 1854,
during the prevalence of cholera, affords no criterion.
It would be well if the Indian Government, whose
duty it is to watch over the interests of the Coolie
emigrants, were to demand from the authorities at
Mauritius an exact return of the mortality among that
class since their first introduction into the colony.   If
this return specified the diseases of which they died,
much useful information might be acquired, and some
preventive measures might be adopted.   The following statement of the mortality among the Coolies
in 1845, 1846, and 1847, said to have been drawn
from official documents, appeared in one of the local
papers:—

					Men.	Women.	Children.
1845	.	.	.	.	1283	127	37
1846	.	.	.	.	797	121	45
1847	.	.	.	.	530	75	13

The Coolie population in the colony, at the close of 1847, is stated in the same paper, to have been 43,865 men, 7355 women, and 3887 children. If these statistics be at all correct, the inference is clear, either that Mauritius is highly unfavourable to the Indian race, or that there are local causes, apart from the influence of climate, producing a large amount of mortality. It is to be hoped that the Indian Government will inquire into this matter. One satisfactory fact is brought to light by the above statements—viz., that during these three years, there was an annual increase in the Coolie population, and an annual decrease in the mortality amongst them, so that the number of deaths in 1847 was less by more than one-half than that of 1845. A large proportion die of fever and of disease of the lungs, brought on by exposure to the different changes in the temperature, during the hours of labour. In the more elevated districts of the colony, the cold drizzly mornings are sufficiently trying to the immigrant newly arrived from the burning plains of Hindostan. It might be supposed, from the paucity of his clothing, that the rain could do him no harm, and might, in fact, have the same good effect as a shower-bath. Experience shews that this opinion is a fallacy. The cold produced by the continued evaporation of the wet from the naked skin, often affects the lungs, and brings on fatal disease. A stranger, observing the half-naked Coolies using umbrellas during the rainy season, is tempted to think either that this is a work of supererogation, or that an umbrella is a badge of respectability. There is in truth something ludicrous in the sight of a man protecting his dress, which consists of a piece of linen drawn tightly round the loins, from the rain with an umbrella. He is not protecting his dress, which would suffer no damage from a thorough drenching, but his skin, the pores of which are apt to admit the cold caused by evaporation.

The favourite article of dress used by the Coolie to protect himself from the cold is a soldier's old coat, the market price of which is one rupee. The shako is appropriated by the ex-apprentices to the adorning of their woolly heads. It is amusing, when there is a slight fall in the thermometer, to witness the troops of Coolies in the streets of Port Louis dressed in this military frippery, and presenting an appearance nearly as grotesque as Falstaff's recruits. Though temperate at their arrival, they soon learn to have recourse to arrack, as a stimulant, which is freely supplied to them at the grog-shops established in the neighbourhood of most of the plantations. The planters usually have shops attached to the estates, similar to those established by the masters in the mining districts in England, where their labourers are supplied with the different articles which they require.

In addition to the free Coolie immigrants employed upon the sugar plantations, there is a large number of their countrymen condemned to labour in the construction or repair of the public roads in Mauritius, as a punishment for the crimes of which they have been found guilty. Indian convicts were first introduced into the colony, under the government of Sir R. T. Farquhar, and were principally Sepoys, who had been guilty of military insubordination or political offences.   Most of these men are now dead.   A few of them are still living at Grand River, exempt from all toil, and supported at the expense of Government.   In physical organisation and general intelligence they are far superior to their Coolie countrymen.   One fine old man, living in the hut nearest to the sea, might sit as a model for one of the patriarchs.   His Oriental features, tall, erect figure, flashing eyes, and flowing beard, recall the pictures of Abraham by the old masters.   He had been a petty officer in a Sepoy regiment, and was banished to the Mauritius for some political offence. Most of the public roads in the colony were constructed by these men, with the assistance of the military.   They worked in chains, under the superintendence of European inspectors, and were lodged in temporary huts near the place of labour.   They bore their exile with all the indifference of their race.   The only crime of which they were known to be guilty, was the murder of one or two of their inspectors, by whom they had been treated with cruelty.

The Coolies employed as domestic servants in the town of Port Louis are different in character from those employed on the estates.   The latter are brought principally from the interior, while the former are the offscourings of the large towns, already drunken, dishonest, and demoralised.   Some of them are Portuguese half-castes, with all the vices peculiar to both the races from which they are sprung.   Drunkenness is their besetting sin.   Many of them are cooks, and their intemperate habits often interfere with their artistic duties in the *cuisine*, and give rise to ludicrous scenes, rather trying to the patience and temper of the lady of the house. We have seen a large party, invited to dinner, waiting, with willing but rather abortive attempts at conversation, for the appearance of the dinner, which did not come. On inquiry, the cook was found drunk and incapable in the kitchen, and the guests were obliged to rest content with such a dinner as the other servants could improvise on the spur of the moment. The drunkenness and dishonesty of their domestic servants, is a subject which rouses even the Creole ladies from their habitual indifference, and makes them in turn eloquent and pathetic about the inconveniences to which they are exposed. Many a sigh of regret is uttered for the good old slavery days, when a lady could sentence a drunken cook to a few dozen of lashes without the intervention of a magistrate, and inflict them with her own hand, if she happened to be of an active disposition, and her taste lay in that direction. The best way to procure good servants is to avoid the former denizens of the large towns of India, and to select them from the peasants of the interior, who are usually sober, honest, and respectful. To be sure you will have to teach them everything, but in this world of mingled good and evil there is no advantage without its inconvenience.

The Coolie servants, on their first arrival, speak only the languages peculiar to the Presidency to which they happen to belong. A few that have been instructed in the missionary institutions, or employed in the families of British residents in India, speak English, but their number is insignificant. The facility and readiness with which the immigrants master the Creole *patois*, within a few weeks after their arrival, argues much in favour of their natural abilities as linguists, and forms a striking contrast to the slow and laborious process by which the less educated British residents, after having spent many years in the colony, are only able to express their simplest wants. This remark applies more particularly to the immigrants resident in Port Louis; those employed on the estates, from having less frequent intercourse with the Creoles, are not so familiar with their language. Many sturdy Britons are indignant that these immigrants should be taught Creole instead of English. In the present circumstances of the colony this result seems to be unavoidable. While an order of the Queen in Council, issued in 1847, made English the official language in all the proceedings of the Government and courts of justice, French, or its *patois* Creole, still continues to be the language spoken by the inhabitants. As the Coolie rarely if ever hears English spoken, he learns Creole, which, though useless to him in India, is more serviceable in Mauritius than English would be. The majority of those employed upon the plantations, having little intercourse with the Creole population, continue to use their native dialects, and receive their orders in the same from the overseers.

The Coolies can scarcely be said to have any religion. The Mohammedan portion of the population have two mosques, one situated near the Trou Fanfaron in Port Louis, and the other at Plaine Verte. The first is a handsome building, in the Moslem style of architecture,

surmounted by a dome, with the entrance protected by
a strong wooden door, covered with symbolic figures,
cut out with considerable skill. The other has been
erected for the accommodation of the followers of Mohammed residing in Malabar Town. The two buildings
could not contain more than three hundred persons, and
the first is attended almost exclusively by the Arab
merchants. These have almost a monopoly of the rice
trade from India, and the money for the erection of the
mosques was raised by imposing a small tax upon every
bag of rice sold by them in the colony. A small building at Grand River has been recently converted into a
mosque. It is attended chiefly by those of the old Sepoy convicts who happen to be followers of the prophet.
The Hindoos have no regular place of worship, and it
may be affirmed, without exaggeration, that the great
mass of the 130,000 Indians in the colony are without
religion of any kind.

There is one great religious festival, if it can be so
called, which is observed once every year by the whole
Indian population, and by some of the lower classes
among the Creoles. It is known in Mauritius as the
Yamseh, and corresponds with the feast of the Mohur-
rum in India. Originally it was celebrated only by the
followers of Mohammed, but now it is regarded as a
sort of general festival, in which all may take part. It is
the rival of the *fête de Dieu* in extravagance and absurdity, and is generally known as the Indian *fête de
Dieu*, to distinguish it from that observed by the Church
of Rome. The Mohammedan world, like the Christian,

is divided into two great sections, each of which claims an exclusive right to orthodoxy, and brands the other with the charge of heresy. It is a sort of question, not of apostolical, but of prophetical succession. Of these two great divisions of the Mohammedan world, the Turks and Arabians recognise Abou Bekir, Omar, and Osman, as the rightful successors of the prophet; while the Persian and Indian Mohammedans denounce these three caliphs as usurpers, and regard Ali, the prophet's son-in-law and minister, as his religious and political heir. This dispute gave rise to a sanguinary contest, in the course of which Hosein, the son of Ali, was attacked near the city of Kerbela by some forces which had been despatched against him. After a brave but unsuccessful resistance, he, along with sixty of his relatives, was massacred on the spot.

The term Yamseh is usually regarded as a corruption of the exclamation used by those who take part in the procession. The Persians and Indians, while taking part in the solemn festival which represents the funeral obsequies of the slaughtered prince, are in the habit of repeating in chorus, " Ya Hosein, O Hosein." The Creoles named the procession from this cry, which was contracted into Yamseh—a word unknown in India, or, in fact, out of Mauritius. This festival is observed during ten or eleven days. At its commencement, the Mohammedans perform their ablutions in the streams nearest to their abodes, and are in the habit of picking up some object while diving, which becomes their *gris-gris*, or charm, till the next festival. Being generally

poor, they have recourse to begging in order to defray
the expenses of the ceremony, which are considerable.
They levy contributions upon all classes, without distinction of rank, race, or religion. At an early hour
in the morning, the begging procession issues from the
Malabar camp, which is situated on the Pamplemousses
road. Those who take part in it have their faces painted, and are dressed in gay, particoloured rags. They
are preceded by a band of performers beating the *tom-
tom*, and making that barbarous noise which the Indians, and they alone, esteem to be music. The leader
of the procession carries in his hand a naked sword,
and is followed by two native priests, bearing aloft a
dish filled with sugar or boiled rice, and covered with
rose leaves. This dish is presented to the occupants of
the different houses which they visit, as a token of
friendship, and an invitation to take part in their religious ceremony, by sharing part of the expense. This
invitation is seldom refused, and while their attendants
are busy collecting the offerings with plates, the mollahs are profuse in their obeisances, *salaams*, and
prayers for the future happiness and prosperity of the
contributors. There is an air of dignity and self-respect in a Mohammedan beggar, amid all his *salaams*,
to which a European professional can never attain.

This money is expended principally in paying the
workmen that have been employed in the construction
of the *gouhn*, which is borne in procession on the great
day of the festival. This *gouhn* is a species of pagoda,
made of bamboo, and covered with tinsel and paper of

different colours. It consists of three storeys, each of which seems to rise from the interior of the other, the one at the base being the largest. The services of the most skilful workmen among the Creoles, Indians, and Chinese are secured for its construction, which sometimes occupies four months. Each storey of the *gouhn* is built in a separate hut, one side of which is knocked down, to allow it to be withdrawn. When the different storeys are completed, they are bound together with strong ligatures, in a fourth hut, large enough to contain the whole pagoda when completed.

On the day before the great day of the Yamseh, the motley population of Malabar Town begins in the evening to pour in a constant tide towards the Plaine Verte, There is the same barbarous music as on the previous days, accompanied with a species of sword-dance, performed by men whose bodies are painted red, intermingled with white and black streaks.

At six o'clock the little procession, as it is called, is formed. The Indians advance bearing on their heads small painted pagodas, in shape and size not unlike a meat-safe, which they call *aïdorès*. These are followed by others armed with clubs and broken swords, with which they attempt to imitate the combat in which Hosein was slain. At a given signal the whole are in motion. The bearers of the *aïdorès* whirl round and round in a fantastic dance with such rapidity that the spectator is almost giddy at the sight. The combatants give and parry blows with wonderful dexterity, uttering at the same time ferocious yells. Others, half-naked and unarmed, are howling and beating their breasts in despair, and rolling in the dust to express their grief at the untimely death of Ali's son. This scene continues till midnight, when they return in the same order to Malabar Town.

Next evening the great procession with which the Yamseh closes takes place. The *gouhn* is brought forth from the hut or temple in which it has been enclosed, and is borne on poles resting on the shoulders of Mozambique negroes, who have been hired for that purpose. These negroes are not followers of Mohammed; they are only worshippers of Mammon. Sometimes, if the contributions have been very liberal, there are two smaller *gouhns*, besides the principal one, which is the great object of attraction. It is not without a sort of barbarous magnificence. The gilt and coloured paper with which its sides are covered is lighted up within by lamps suspended from the roof, and without by paper lanterns attached to every angle and pinnacle of its pointed architecture, like the lights attached to the branches of a Christmas-tree. These lanterns are shaken by the movements of the bearers, and their flickering light is reflected from the gilt sides of the *gouhn*, giving it at times the dazzling appearance of a temple of solid gold. It is preceded by a sort of torchbearers, who carry at the end of long poles illuminated lanterns of glass, representing the sun, the crescent, and certain of the stars. The procession moves with slow and solemn step, regulated by the monotonous dirge-like chant of the mollahs. The *aïdorès* are

whirled in the air with the same rapidity as the bodies
of their bearers, the sword combats are resumed, the
mourners beat their breasts, and the whole air resounds
with mournful shouts, "Yah Hosein! O Hosein!"
Besides the pagoda representing Hosein's funeral-car,
there are other figures in the procession, symbolical of
events connected with his death. His last struggle is
represented with death-like fidelity by a bull-necked
Malabar, who dies with an artistic neatness which
Macready might envy. The lion that watched for several days over the sacred remains of Ali's slaughtered son
finds a representative in a broad-chested follower of the
prophet, whose naked skin is painted in imitation of a
lion's tawny hide. He utters the most fearful bellow-
ings, and from time to time makes a rush at the crowd,
which retreats before him. His onsets are restrained
by the cord with which his keeper leads him along,
and by certain mysterious words and magnetic passes,
used by the priest that accompanies him. The devil,
rejoicing at Hosein's death, appears in the form of a
mountebank, who leaps surprising distances into the
air, waving his arms wildly round his head, and hissing
like a serpent.

After the procession has traversed the principal
streets of Port Louis, it directs its march towards the
Lataniers River, followed by thousands of spectators,
some on foot, others in carriages. The Lataniers
River is only worthy of that name in the rainy season;
in summer it is only a small rivulet flowing through
the Vallée des Prêtres. At midnight the procession

halts at a pool, a short way above the bridge on the Pamplemousses road, the *gouhn* is lighted at its four corners, and dropped into the water. Only its lower part is immersed in the water, and the flames spread rapidly from storey to storey, till they rise above it in a fiery volume, which sheds its flickering light upon the upturned countenances of the spectators, which exhibit a richness and variety of colour such as no artist could represent on canvas. At length the flame dies out, and the crowd disperses—the Creoles to discuss the events of the day, the Coolies to feast upon boiled rice and curried cocks, the approved dish on the occasion of the Yamseh. These fowls, sacred to the slaughtered Hosein, and savoury to the Mohammedan palate, which has tasted no solid food for days, have either been surreptitiously removed by the Coolies from the roosts of their infidel masters, or have been contributed by their Creole neighbours, who, while professing Christianity after a sort, think that a cock bestowed upon the prophet may not be altogether lost. For the same politic reason, the Yezzids worship the principle of evil. This miserable exhibition of heathenism is tolerated, if not countenanced, by the local Government. All vehicles are prohibited from passing by the *route* pursued by the Yamseh procession, and the police attend to preserve order.

Apart from all religious considerations, this festival has a demoralising influence upon the Coolie population. It unhinges and unsettles their minds, and makes them averse to their usual employments. It often leads them to desert their employment and to rob their masters, who are often obliged to fast during the Yamseh, without the merit of voluntary abstinence. The cook often disappears, carrying with him the *batterie de cuisine*, and the raw material for the manufacture of a Yamseh supper. Such is his grief for the death of Hosein that he seldom returns, except it be to console himself with the contents of his master's plate-chest.

The Yamseh can scarcely be regarded as a religious festival, or as an indication of the religious faith of those who take part in it. Of Mohammedan origin, it is now observed by Hindoos and Mohammedans without distinction. A recent event affords a striking proof of the religious indifference that has sprung up among this portion of the population. For the last two years, the *gouhns*, instead of being cast into the stream and burned, as Mohammedan orthodoxy demands, have been rescued from fire and water, and preserved to take part in the procession of the ensuing year. This fact may seem trivial in itself. It shews, however, that faith is dying out among the followers of the prophet, as well as among others, and that the spirit of commerce is stronger than the spirit of fanaticism. There is reason to believe that the Coolie population has deteriorated, and lapsed into crime, in the absence of those restraining influences which every religion, however bad, must present. Every religion must embody a certain amount of truth, to which it owes its existence as a religion at all. That truth must exercise a certain influence for good upon all who believe it. Mohammedanism, with all its fanaticism and sensuality—Hinduism, with all its idolatry and impurity, are better than the absence or negation of all religion, which implies also the absence or negation of all those influences for good which the truth embodied in each of these systems can exercise. The condition of the Coolies in Mauritius, without any religion, is more deplorable, so far as their moral character is concerned, than if they retained their original faith. There can be no doubt, however, but that it presents greater facilities for their Christianisation. Half of the missionary's work is already done. He has not to destroy the edifice, and then to rebuild it upon another foundation. It is already in ruins.

The state of practical atheism into which the Coolie population has fallen, cannot be otherwise than favourable to the progress of crime. The worst religion has a certain restraining influence over its adherents; and it is a dangerous condition for any community, when a large portion of its inhabitants have cast off their old faith, without receiving any substitute. No doubt this condition cannot be permanent. It is only a transition state. Man is so constituted that he cannot live long in the negation of all religion, and must have something positive to believe in. The history of the first French Revolution places this fact beyond a doubt. The Coolies cannot remain long in their present condition. Unless a strenuous effort be made by the Protestant Church at home to send missionaries to instruct them in the simple truths of the gospel, like the coloured population of Mauritius at the time of the emancipation, they will fall into the hands of the Church of Rome. That Church has done nothing for them as yet: she has had her hands full with the Creole population, which had a prior claim upon her attention. It is only of late years that the Protestant Churches in the colony have begun to bestir themselves in this matter. The Church of Scotland took the initiative, but her adherents in the colony, though deeply interested in this question, are not so numerous as to be able to do much in the missionary field, unless they be aided by the parent Church at home.

Next to the absence of religion, the greatest cause of crime among the Coolie population is the paucity of women. Among Orientals, unaccustomed to restrain their passions, and deprived of those influences that teach the exercise of self-control, this must ever be a fertile source of crime. The Coolie estimate of the value of human life is not high, and when the passion of jealousy is excited, it often leads to murder. With the increase of population there must naturally be an increase of crime, and the amount of crime committed by the Coolies is not greater than might be expected under the circumstances in which they are placed. The increase in the number of murders, committed generally from motives of jealousy, has been so great of late years, that the interference of the Home Government is imperatively demanded. The only cure for this evil is a more equal proportion of the two sexes among the Coolie immigrants introduced into Mauritius. Murder is not the only evil resulting from the present disproportion ; there are crimes of a different nature, which cannot be specified.

The proportion of females introduced with the first immigrants was very small. Only 200 females accompanied 10,000 males, so that there was only one woman for every fifty males. According to the census of 1846, the Indian population amounted to 48,935 males, and 7310 females, or about one woman for every seven men. According to the census of 1851, the whole population of Mauritius amounted to 120,331 males, and 64,482 females ; but, from the progress of agriculture and the increased importation of Coolie labourers since 1851, the population at the present moment cannot be less than 230,000, of whom about 130,000 are natives of India. The disproportion between the sexes among the Creole population is comparatively smaller. There is about one-sixth fewer females than males. If the present population of Mauritius, exclusive of the Coolies, be estimated at 100,000, the number of females belonging to the general population will be about 42,000. When this number is deducted from the 64,482 females belonging to all classes in 1851, and a certain allowance made for the increase of female immigrants since that period, an estimate may be formed of the present proportion of the sexes among the Coolie population. There are about 25,000 Indian women among 105,000 men, or about one woman for every four men. While this calculation shews an increase in the number of Indian females since 1846, it proves at the same time that there is still a great disproportion between the sexes, which cannot but be productive of much immorality and crime. The frequency of murders committed under the influence of jealousy has directed the attention of the local authorities to this subject. The evil in all its extent is fully recognised, but the sole remedy that can check it, the introduction of more women, and of a better class than those now in the island, has not yet been adopted. The Indian women in the colony are of the very worst class, and the agents in India, instead of sending the present class of women, should take care that the female emigrants are really the wives of those whom they accompany. A little more care in the selection of these women would do much to ameliorate the moral condition of the Coolies, and to diminish those crimes that have become so frequent of late years. The evil, however, can only be remedied by increasing the female emigrants, till they bear something like the same proportion to the male population, as the same class among the Creoles. Such a measure would not only tend to repress crime, but would also aid very much in checking that desertion of employment of which the planters complain; and in establishing a permanent resident Coolie population, which would make the island independent of the annual emigration from India. So long as the Coolie labourer, or in truth any labourer, has no local ties to bind him to a place, no woman that he can call his wife, and no house that he can call his home, he will be restless, wandering and fond of change, immoral in his habits and prone to crime.

The facilities for missionary labour presented by the

present abnormal condition of the Coolies, have been already alluded to, and it is deeply to be regretted that the Protestant Churches at home, in concentrating all their efforts upon the heathen in India, have overlooked the claims of the same class in Mauritius. No doubt, India is the stronghold of heathenism, before which the battle of the cross must be fought and won ; but Mauritius is one of those outposts, the capture of which would contribute much to the final overthrow of that stronghold. The Coolies in Mauritius come from the different parts of the three Presidencies, some of which are so remote as to be beyond the pale of missionary enterprise. After the expiry of their engagement, many of them return to the places of their birth, enlightened in almost everything save the one thing needful. If these men were instructed in Christianity, they might convey to their heathen countrymen the seeds of divine truth, and prepare the way for the advent of the missionary. Through their travels and the wealth which they have acquired, they command a certain amount of respect among their countrymen, who would be prepared to listen more favourably to the gospel proclaimed by them than by missionaries imperfectly acquainted with their language and feelings. At the present moment, when England is still thrilling at the recital of the horrors that heathenism has perpetrated upon her sons and daughters, and is seeking to retaliate as a Christian nation, by bringing the gospel to bear upon the native population with accumulated force, the importance of

Mauritius as a missionary field ought not to be overlooked. There is constant intercourse between this
island and the continent, and almost every ship that
sails for India conveys immigrants to their native land.
These men, while liberated from the bonds of traditional
superstition, remain as ignorant of Christianity as before. No effort has been made to instruct them, and
their influence upon their heathen countrymen is lost.
Native labour may be one of the great means through
which the evangelisation of India is to be effected.
There is much in the past history of missionary labour
in that country to lead to this conclusion.   At least, no
means that seem to have any probability of success
ought to be overlooked.   If it could be even shewn that
the Christianisation of the Coolies in Mauritius can
have no influence upon the evangelisation of their
countrymen in India, the duty of making known the
gospel to them would still remain the same.   They have
not the same prejudices of caste as their countrymen in
India, and are almost prepared to accept any form of
religion that may be offered to them.   Their moral and
religious condition is thus alluded to in a local publication, issued in 1854, and the truthfulness of the statement which it contains has never been questioned :—

"There are in Mauritius at the present moment
upwards of a hundred thousand Indian immigrants,
almost entirely destitute of religious instruction, deprived of caste, liberated from the bonds of native
superstition, uncontrolled by any moral restraint,
ripe for almost every crime.   Recent circumstances

prove that this is no exaggerated picture. Hitherto, we have been satisfied with their manual labour, without looking to their moral condition, till the progress of crime has forced this subject on the notice of every thinking man. All admit the disease; the only question is as to the remedy. The disease may be complex, the remedy may require to partake of the same character. The extension and better organisation of the established means for detecting and punishing crime—the compulsory education, if necessary, of all the offspring of Indian parents, at the expense of Government or of their employers—and greater firmness on the part of the Executive in carrying into effect the sentences of the law;—such are the means usually suggested for stemming the rapidly increasing flow of Indian crime. Without questioning the utility of these as subsidiary measures, the Committee believe that they can only affect the surface of the disease, without reaching to the secret principle which is the cause of all the evil, and which is to be sought for in the natural depravity of the human heart when unenlightened by divine revelation, and unrestrained by the knowledge of a judgment to come. The law of the Lord alone is perfect, converting the soul. Human laws may punish crime, but they cannot produce virtue; measures of restraint may divert the course, but they cannot arrest the progress of the evil. While the fountain remains, the stream will not cease to flow. It is now as in the days of Elisha the son of Shaphat—the salt must be cast into the spring, the Lord must heal the waters, so as that there shall not be from thence any more death."*

The recent circumstances alluded to in this Report were several aggravated cases of murder among the Indians, and the death of torture inflicted upon an old lady, a native of the colony. Among the atrocities committed in the Indian mutiny, there has no case been revealed where greater ingenuity and diabolical skill in torturing the victim were exhibited. The cupidity of her servants had been excited by the belief that she had a large sum of money in the house. This money had been removed to a place of safety. Ignorant of this, her servants, with their associates, formed a plan to rob and murder her. They met at a house in Moka Street, and fortified themselves for the work in hand by a hearty supper and copious draughts of arrack. Twelve of them found their way into the solitary house which she occupied in Rempart Street. What followed is known only from their confession after their conviction. They found the lady in bed, and demanded her money. She said, truly, that it had been removed. This was denied by her servants, and they proceeded to torture her. For four hours their victim was exposed to sufferings such as cannot be described. At the end of that time she died beneath their hands, and their cupidity was defeated. The cool deliberate cruelty of the Hindoo character is shewn by the fact, that while their victim was undergoing her sufferings, her persecutors were enjoying themselves by drinking her champagne.

* Bible Society Report.

The crimes of the Indians, however, rarely extend beyond themselves. This is the only case where, of late years, a white person has been murdered by the Coolies. The murders that are committed among themselves usually arise from two motives—jealousy and cupidity. Jealousy is a frequent source of crime in India : its power must be much more intense in a colony where the disproportion between the sexes is so great. The women are a most immoral class, and often become the victims of their own misconduct and of their husbands' jealousy. Their foolish fondness of display is another frequent cause of murder. The rupees gained by their husbands are manufactured by native jewellers into ornaments for the nose, ears, neck, arms, and ankles. When these parts of the body are loaded with silver till they can bear no more, a new species of jewel is worn. A small clasp of gold is attached to a sovereign, which is worn round the neck with a ribbon. On all public occasions these ornaments are ostentatiously displayed, and their dusky wearers are often murdered, or made insensible by the administration of stromnium, in which state they are stripped of their jewels. The victims are sometimes enticed or carried into the canefields, to places little frequented, where their bodies are found at the cutting of the crop, in such a state of decomposition that it is sometimes impossible to identify them.

From the removal of the two regiments stationed in the colony during the Indian insurrection, and the character of the Coolies employed on the plantations, serious fears were at one time entertained that they might endeavour to imitate the example of their countrymen. Subsequent experience proved that these fears were groundless. A few inflammatory addresses to the Mohammedan population, issued by their mollahs, excited but little notice, and were speedily removed by the police. The Coolies, being undisciplined and unaccustomed to the use of fire-arms, would not have been a very formidable foe. There is no reason, however, to suspect their loyalty. If there had been a Sepoy regiment in the colony, and the English soldiers removed, there might have been an attempt at insurrection, which the discipline of the police and the bravery of the planters would, no doubt, have speedily suppressed.

Among the Coolies resident in Port Louis there are about a hundred that have been educated in Protestant Missionary Institutions, and made a profession of Christianity in their native land. These men, on their arrival in the colony, were at once surrounded by all the seductive influences of sin, without any agency to counteract these influences. They had no pastoral superintendence and no place of worship. That under such circumstances many of them should have relapsed into those sinful habits which are common among their heathen countrymen, need excite no surprise. Such a fact can afford no argument against the value of missionary labours, or the fitness of the Hindoo for the reception of Christianity. It might as well be inferred that, because many natives of the British Isles now resident in Mauritius, after having been once admitted into the Church through baptism, have now relapsed into a state of practical infidelity, the labours of ministers at home are useless, and Christianity not adapted to the Anglo-Saxon race. Such a fact proves merely that human nature, amid all the distinctions of colour and race, is essentially the same, and that men, however sincere their belief in Christianity may be, are ever apt to relapse into practical error, when removed from those influences which alone can retain them in the way of truth. It is melancholy to contrast the prayerful labour and anxious care bestowed upon these men before they made a profession of Christianity in India, with the utter absence of all the means of grace, and the all but certain apostasy, to which they are exposed in Mauritius. None of them have really renounced Christianity, or resumed the profession of heathenism, though most of them retain nothing of Christianity save the name. The best educated amongst them were trained by the Rev. J. Anderson, senior member of the Free Church Mission, Madras, one of the most successful labourers that Scotland has ever contributed to the missionary cause. He is now beyond the reach of all human praise; but it is gratifying to find that, "he being dead, yet speaketh," and that the echo of his voice is still heard in the islands of the Indian Ocean. In Mauritius, as well as in Bourbon, there are natives of India, now reclaimed to Christianity, who bless the memory of him to whom they were indebted for their first knowledge of divine truth.

The merit of the first successful inroad upon Coolie

heathenism in Mauritius is due to the Committee of
the Madras Bible Society.   The circumstances under
which it was made are related in their Report for 1855.
After stating that a large sum had been raised for the
Jubilee Fund, and reserved for special appropriation by
the Committee, the Report proceeds :—" Anticipating
the hearty concurrence of the Home Committee, and
thinking it desirable that no time should be lost in making some provision for the spiritual wants of the Coolie
immigrants in Mauritius, your Committee resolved
to despatch two agents to that island, furnished with a
large supply of Scriptures.   Mr A. Taylor and John
Baptist, the two persons selected for the work, sailed
in the month of June (1854), in the ship *Anna Maria.*
Your Committee were not aware, at the time of their
agents leaving Madras, of the existence of an Auxiliary
Bible Society at the Mauritius, or they would gladly
have availed themselves of the Committee's help in the
carrying out of their views for the welfare of the immigrants.   The best arrangement they could make under
the circumstances, was to request their friend and
fellow-labourer, the Rev. J. Hardey, then providentially
detained on the island, and well acquainted with the
Tamil language, to undertake the superintendence of the
agents ; and in the event of his having left, to com-
mend them to the kind care and supervision of the
Rev. L. Banks, who had for a long time manifested a
lively interest in the immigrants.   Great was your Committee's disappointment to learn that, on the arrival of
their agents at the sphere of labour, Mr Hardey had

gone, and that Mr Banks had been removed by that desolating scourge, cholera. In this emergency, the Rev. P. Beaton, Secretary of the Mauritius Bible Society, appeared. He kindly introduced the agents to the Committee there, and has ever since shewn a lively interest in their work." Mr Hardey, the missionary from Madras, to whom allusion is made in the above extract, had, during his residence in the colony, organised a small congregation of Tamullian Christians, who used to assemble at his house on Sundays for worship. These men had been converted to Christianity in India, and called upon Mr Hardey, as soon as they knew that he was acquainted with the Tamil language. The average attendance at his Sunday service was about thirty adults, or one-half of the Tamullian Christians resident in Port Louis. The others were living such sinful lives as led them to avoid all intercourse with the missionary. After his departure, his small congregation was dispersed, there being no minister in the colony acquainted with the Tamil language. Mr Taylor, one of the agents from Madras, a well-educated and intelligent Eurasian, resumed the service in the Tamil language. A better idea of the moral and religious condition of the Coolies may be derived from extracts from his quarterly Reports, than from any vague or general description of their manners. Mr Taylor entered upon his labours about the middle of July 1854. On the 12th of October, he writes—

"To convey a clear idea of the impression that has been made on the minds of the Tamullians generally in this town, I have only to state, that what I have witnessed has often filled my heart with devout gratitude to the Lord, for His gracious presence and blessing on our work, and I am thankful also to add, that the favourable impression made on the minds of many heathen and Romanists does not seem to wear away, as the novelty of our operations begins to subside, but that, in most cases, those who once attended with apparent interest to the gospel have continued to manifest the same feeling towards it, and many of them even expressed their intention to attend our Sunday services; and, although this has been done by only a few comparatively, yet I can unhesitatingly state that, if the impression already made on the minds of many heathens and Romanists, in this town alone, be vigorously followed up, great results may reasonably be hoped for. You will be rejoiced also to know that this opinion has been expressed by some respectable Romanists, and that some of the heathen have said to us, that many among themselves would prefer our religion to that of the Romanists, who wanted heavy fees for burials, &c.

"You are already aware that *caste*, although existing here in a certain degree, does not present any serious impediment to the embracing of Christianity by the heathen; and as to the difficulties arising from family connexions, these also seem to have but little influence among them, as many are known to live together as husband and wife where the parties are of different *castes*. In reference to inducements to continue in idolatry, I must mention that, though there has been, for the last three or four years, an insignificant temple about two miles from Port Louis, and though a site for another has already been engaged, the foundation of which is to be laid at an early period, yet, as there are only about five Brahmins in this colony, and these held in disrepute by the people generally, they are not likely to give that stimulus to idolatry which is necessary to excite the people to continue in the observance of its usages and ceremonies.

"As to the Romanists, I have to state that, with the exception of a few of the older inhabitants, and the descendants of some who emigrated to the island before the British came into possession of it, all of whom, therefore, are acquainted with a little French, they are absolutely without a priest to minister to them in the Tamil language ; so that some of them, on hearing of my arrival, and mistaking me for a Romanist, expressed great joy that now at last the opportunity of making auricular confession and receiving absolution was about to be offered to them. You will, therefore, not be surprised to hear that the Romanists in this colony do not manifest any bitterness of feeling against us, and that they have not only purchased copies of the whole Bible and of the New Testament, but that in many instances they willingly listen to the Word of God, as has frequently been the case when I proposed to read it to them in some of the houses of the respectable Romanists. And more than this, what will please you not a little is the fact, that some of them, including two or three respectable persons, have attended our Sunday services, and are likely to become permanently connected with us. I must further mention, that even a few, who appeared a little shy of us at the first, are now shewing a more friendly feeling, and even speaking of coming to our Sunday worship. In regard to the distribution of the Scriptures, you will be rejoiced to hear that twenty-six copies of the Tamil Bible, three complete copies of the Old Testament, thirty-six (one-fourth) parts of the Old Testament, twenty-eight New Testaments, and eight diglotts, have been sold. Although the above, considered in itself, may not appear a large number, yet when the fact that the greater part has been purchased by Romanists and heathen, who till then had not perhaps seen a copy of the Word of God, is taken into account, it must appear to be a matter of sincere thankfulness to the Lord that He has sent His Word into the houses of so many that have been sitting in darkness and in the valley of the shadow of death. As to the smaller portions of the Scriptures which are given away gratuitously, so many have been distributed among Tamullians who were able to read, and appeared anxious to have them, that we cannot state the number with any probability of correctness." After citing several cases, which prove that the Coolies are anxious to possess the Word of God, and prepared to make considerable sacrifices to obtain copies of it, Mr Taylor continues—" In reference to our Sunday services, I have to state, that the attendance has been gradually increasing from six or seven adults (at the forenoon service) on the first, second, or third Sundays, to twenty-two adults on the first of this month. I am happy also to add, that of the number just mentioned eight or nine were heathen. In connexion with this, I think I could safely say that, if a chapel were built in some conspicuous place (as our house is not situated in a central position), the attendance on Sundays is likely to be larger. The want of proper seats is also much felt, as the Tamullians and other immigrants have adopted the European costume and habits ; and also as a few of the respectable portion of hearers, not liking to be jammed up with the lower orders, appear to be uncomfortable.

" You are already aware that there are from fifty to sixty (Tamullian) Protestants in this town, and may, therefore, be surprised to find that the attendance at our Sunday worship is not larger. I must account for this by mentioning the following facts—namely, that the Lord's day is not generally observed in this town as a day of sacred rest, but as one of recreation, and consequently household servants find it hard to obtain permission to attend the means of grace ; and secondly, not a few of the Protestants have fallen into the habit of drunkenness, which is very prevalent here, and some are living in open adultery. These persons are, consequently, anxious to avoid us as much as possible.

" You will thus perceive that the Lord has opened up a wide door for making known the gospel to thousands of souls in this colony, and that a favourable opportunity to commence a mission presents itself here, which the Lord, no doubt, will put into the hearts of His faithful people to endeavour to do without any further delay."

In the course of the first year, 2750 Scriptures, or portions of Scripture, in the Tamil language, were sold or distributed among the immigrants from the Madras Presidency. A more favourable field for this species of labour than Mauritius cannot exist. A large proportion of the Indian immigrants can read; the coating of *caste* is rubbed off by the friction of a sea voyage; and the Coolie of Mauritius, through constant contact with other races, has his mind expanded, and soon becomes intellectually superior to the same class in India. He receives a fair reward for his labour, and learns to respect himself as an integral part of the body politic. His reasoning powers are far more largely developed than those of his African neighbours; he is, therefore, less apt to become the dupe of Romish superstition. He has a certain ambition in life, and knows the value of money; he is, therefore, less willing to expend it in fees to the Romish priesthood. The African is ready to become the slave of any one that will take the trouble to bind the fetters upon his soul and his body. Britain has liberated his body, but Rome retains his soul. Rome knows her power, and where that power may be exercised with effect. She has drawn the African within her coils, and found him an unresisting victim, but she has left the Coolie alone. The Indian intellect is too subtle to present a favourable soil for the reception of the seeds of Romanism. The Indian is guided by reason, the

African is led by his imagination. The Church of Rome addresses herself to the imagination by her pompous rites and imposing ceremonies, and thus possesses a power of attraction to the African mind to which Protestantism can lay no claim. But the Indian is made to be a Protestant, just because he is a thinking, reasoning being, who will admit no doctrine unless he can give a reason for it, and perceive its connexion with other truths. No one who has undertaken to impart religious instruction to Indians and Africans can fail to have been struck with the keen dialectical power of the one race, and the blind, unreasoning credulity of the other.

CHAPTER VI.

Arrival of the Rev. David Fenn—His Interest in the Coolie Mission—
Mr Taylor's Second Report—Attempt to Identify Protestantism
with Freemasonry — The Freemasons Excommunicated by the
Roman Catholic Bishop—Coolies neglected by the Church of Rome
—Causes of this Neglect—Connexion between Mauritius as a Mis-
sionary Field, and the Future Evangelisation of India—Deplorable
condition of Christian Coolies—Mr Taylor's Third Report—Arrival
of the Bishop of Mauritius—Mr Taylor's Ordination—John Baptist
—Service for Bengalee Immigrants—Amusing Anecdote of an
Indian Servant—Coolie Colporteurs—Good Effected by Reading the
Scriptures—Striking proof of this—Honesty of Christian Servants
—Antipathy against them—Coolie Children Uneducated—An Ex-
perimental School—Its Failure, and the Cause—Mauritius as a
Field for Coolie Education—A Native School—Success of Experi-
mental School—Government Ordinance enforcing Education.

IN 1854, a young and devoted missionary, intimately
acquainted with the Tamil language, visited Mauritius,
for the purpose of recruiting his health, which had
been injured through over-exertion and the effects of
the climate of India. This was the Rev. David Fenn,
who had been sent out by the Church of England
Missionary Society to labour in the Madras Presidency.
After his arrival in Mauritius, he manifested a lively interest in the efforts that were being made to bring the
truths of the gospel within the reach of the Coolies in
the colony; and while the delicate state of his health
prevented him from undertaking so much as he would

have wished, his advice and experience were very valuable, and he kindly aided Mr Taylor in his missionary labours among the Tamullians. It was not to be expected that the mass of heathenism in the colony should be leavened all at once with the leaven of Divine truth, or that the devoted labours of the two or three agents at work should produce all at once any very perceptible results. They had to labour and to wait in prayerful expectation, that the seed sown might take root and bring forth fruit. Nor was such fruit wanting. There was enough of it to justify them in believing that the Word of God was stirring the dry bones of heathenism, and preparing the way for the future labours of such men as God should raise up to enter in and take possession of the field, and complete the good work which they had begun. Mr Taylor's able and interesting Reports shed much light upon the workings of the Coolie mind, and the obstacles that are opposed to the progress of Christianity amongst them. On the 15th of January 1855, he writes:—

"In reviewing the operations and results of the last quarter, I am led to feel deeply thankful to the Lord for His continued presence with me in my labours. It will be very gratifying to you to know, that after the expiration of six months the attention of both heathen and Romanists to the Word of God has not diminished in the least, and that throughout the town generally there is a favourable impression in regard to it. As a proof of the readiness with which they hear the message of salvation, I would mention that on many occasions they have offered me a small present in money, which I of course have always refused. Even a few Mohammedans have received our books, and appear to have lost that violent zeal for their own religion which they manifest in India. And the desire to receive our books is so general, that the Bengal immigrants have frequently applied for books in Magarree, as well as in the different languages spoken in that Presidency. You will also be pleased to hear that people who have purchased or received books from us have taken them into the country, where also a slight movement has been produced by them ; and what will be peculiarly gratifying to you is a fact that has come to my knowledge, viz., that two Protestants, having between them three complete copies of the Tamil Bible, have taken them to the neighbouring Island of Bourbon. In illustration of what I have said, I will give you a few extracts from my journal for the present month, to shew the state of feeling still manifested by heathens and Romanists:—

"'5th January 1855.—While passing near the market I spoke to a Romanist who appears favourably disposed in reference to the gospel. When I was speaking to him, a Coolie said to me, that he would shew me a man who was able to read, and asked me to accompany him a few yards. He brought me to a group of eight or ten Coolies near the wharf. I commenced to address them, and some others gathered round me. Some of them, who had heard me before, said that they had been talking among themselves about coming to our Sunday services. After I reached home, I found a heathen, who has attended our services on six or seven occasions, waiting to speak to me. He said he wanted a book, which would give him a clear idea of Christian doctrines. I gave him a Gospel of Luke and a copy of an Elementary Catechism.'

" ' *6th January.*—Spoke in five different places this morning. In one of these, met a man who said he had been twelve years on the island, but had never before heard that God had sent His Son to save a lost world. He appeared very glad at what I said, and promised to come and see me in my house, to become better acquainted with Christianity.'

" ' *9th.*—Went to " Kakamoodoo" this morning, and spoke in a certain place to five or six Tamullians, who were most of them very attentive. One of them pressed me to accept a small piece of money. I of course refused it, and said that the only thing I required of him was to lay seriously to heart the importance of the truths I had made known to him. Then went to Ismal's house. The woman with whom he is living (and who wants to be baptized), though very unwell under the effects of a fever, came out of her house and sat in the yard to hear us. I read to her and to Narramsamy, (a man living in Ismal's house) the first ten verses of the fifth chapter of Matthew, and spoke to them for more than half-an-hour. I next went to that part of the village where I have most hearers. I here made the Romanist to whom I had given a copy of the Gospel of Luke some time ago, read the parable of the prodigal son to me. There were about five others also listening. After he had finished, I expounded it to others, and they seemed to feel some interest in what they heard.'

"'11*th January.*—Went to a bazaar in Malabar Town, and spoke to six persons. The owner of the bazaar was particularly attentive, and when his assistant wanted to put me a question, he said to him, "Shut your mouth ; you 'll now propose a rude question in your usual rude manner." The man, however, promising to say nothing but what was allowable, proposed his question. It was this, Whether God was not alike the author of sin as of virtue ? My answer seemed to satisfy them all, and the man who proposed the question also asked for a book. He had received a copy of the Acts of the Apostles from me some time ago, and I was informed by the owner of the bazaar, that only the preceding day something that he had read in it had become the subject of discussion between them, which appeared to me to be the reason of the latter trying to stop him when he was about proposing the question above mentioned.'

"After what I have said, you will be naturally led to inquire, whether any more apparent result has been produced by the Word of God than the mere assent to the truth of Christianity. It rejoices me to be able to answer this question in the affirmative, although at the same time I would speak guardedly, lest I should appear to be anxious to give a varnish to facts which in themselves may not be worthy of particular notice. I would, therefore, only state that among the heathens who have, on different occasions, expressed a desire to embrace Christianity, there are at present at least six individuals, of whom I have reason to believe that the impression made upon their minds is not a mere momentary one, as they have not only constantly attended our Sunday services, but are also receiving instruction from me with a view to baptism. My sincere prayer therefore is, that they may not prove to be either stony ground or thorny ground hearers.

" In reference to the Romanists, I have to state that a great many of the poorer sort appear to have no knowledge of the difference existing between their Church and our own, and that not a few of them appear willing to attend our Sunday services, and allege their extra work on the Lord's day as the only reason of their not doing so. And, although there have been a few instances of Romanists refusing to receive copies of the smaller portions of Scripture, on the ground of their being of a different creed, yet most of them, after being shewn the importance of every professing Christian becoming acquainted with the truths of revelation, have been persuaded to accept copies of the Gospels and Acts, and even to purchase the larger portions. In connexion with the above, I must also state that I observed an effort made, soon after our arrival, to mislead the poor ignorant Romanists, by making out a connexion between Protestants and Freemasons, who are represented to be guilty of the most fearful crimes; owing to which some were deterred from hearing us, but I

am happy to state, that I have not lately heard anything which savoured of that unfavourable impression.
I am therefore still of opinion, as stated in my first
Report, that if a chapel were built which all could easily
find, many of the Romanists, as well as heathen, would
be induced to assemble in it on the Lord's day, more
especially as not a few of both classes have told me,
when I have seen them in different parts of the town,
that they had come in search of my house, but could
not find it.

"I have further to state, that some of the heathen
whom I have met appear to have received favourable
impressions with regard to Christianity in the several
places in India from which they have come, and that
among them are a great many youths and men in ma-
ture age who have been educated in mission schools in
Tranquebar.

"Another pleasing fact which I must bring to your
notice is, that some of the heathen who have heard
me, and received books from me, have not only gone
and spoken favourably of Christianity to their friends
and acquaintances, whom I had not seen, but have also
induced them to come for books, and even to attend
our Sunday services. And you will be glad to hear,
that when I have been sometimes interrupted (which is
very seldom) in my street-preaching by a drunkard or
one disposed to cavil, the rest of my hearers, so far from
being pleased at it, or disposed to join against me,
have endeavoured to silence the individual who opposed,
either by answering for me or by requesting him to

listen quietly, telling him they were anxious to hear what I was saying. And in some shops and bazaars I have been so well received, that I have been not only permitted to read or speak for half-an-hour at a time, but I have also had the happiness of making the owner read a whole chapter to me, and even two or three chapters on some occasions, besides listening to my remarks on the same.

"In reference to our Sunday services, it will be gratifying to you to hear, that the average attendance at the forenoon's service during last month was thirty adults; on one Sunday during that month there were thirty-five present, of these two were obliged to sit in an adjoining room from want of space in that in which the services are held. On the same day, three others, who could not come before, came a little after the service was over, and another man, seeing how the room was crowded, went away without attempting to find a place. Besides these, a man who came much too early did not wait until the service commenced. So that there were altogether forty persons who came from various distances *expressly* to attend our worship. Thus, you will perceive, that our out-door work is having a good effect on some heathens and Romanists, who form about one-third of our congregation on Sundays. I must not omit to mention that Mr Fenn kindly conducted some of the Sunday evening services during the months of November and December, and that he has also administered baptism to two children belonging to the congregation.

"Among the Protestants, or nominal Christians, I am thankful to observe that there appear to be some signs of life among those who attend our services, although I have still to complain that a great many of them continue to keep aloof from us. Of these some appear to be irreclaimably sunk in sin and vice, and others appear happy to find an excuse in the well-known fact of the disregard of the Sabbath manifested by their employers. In connexion with this part of my subject, I have to lament the disproportion of females among the immigrants as a sad cause of evil, not only among the heathen but also among the Protestants.

"Before bringing this to a close, I will just allude to a subject which I have no doubt must have occurred to the minds of Christians in India, viz., that the preaching of the gospel in this colony to the heathen is calculated under God to have a salutary effect in the several places to which the emigrants who have spent their time return, as many do every year. Under this impression I have frequently visited the Emigration Depôt, and spoken to groups waiting there to be sent back to India."

The allusion in this Report to the attempt made to confound Protestantism with Freemasonry, requires some explanation. At this period the Roman Catholic Bishop had commenced a crusade against those members of his Church who had been initiated into the mysteries of Freemasonry. There are two lodges at Port Louis, the one patronised by the white and the other by the coloured population. Freemasonry has struck its roots deep into the Mauritius soil—deeper, as the event proved, than Romanism. It ranks among its adherents almost the whole male population that have received a liberal education, or occupy a respectable position in life. It has its secrets, known only to the initiated, its social meetings, its annual balls, and its munificent charities. It is the rival of Romanism, or at least it came to be regarded in that light. The principal lodge is situated close to the Bishop's palace. His slumbers may have been disturbed by the sound of revelry by night, or his episcopal fears excited by observing that the Creole population became bad Romanists in proportion as they became good masons; whatever the cause may have been, the fact is certain—he resolved to suppress Freemasonry. He refused the ordinances of religion to all Freemasons who did not renounce that system. He proved by the clearest and most irresistible logic, that Freemasonry being denounced by Romanism, no Romanist could be a Freemason, and no Freemason could be treated as a member of the Church. His conduct was as consistent as his logic; he made no distinction between the rich and the poor — he refused to all alike the sacraments of their faith until they abjured Freemasonry, and were re-admitted into the Church.* Throughout the whole of this

* Mass was recently performed at Nôtre Dame for the souls of the Freemasons who died excommunicated. What are we to believe? That the souls of the masons are still *in limbo*, or that the Mass opened a door for their escape? Be that as it may, it is clear that Romanism is one thing at Mauritius and another at Paris, and that the unity of the Church of Rome exists only in theory.

affair, he shewed a clearness of intellect, a strength
of will, and steadfastness of purpose, that did not fail
to excite the admiration of those who had no sympathy
with his tenets, and little interest in the question at
issue. The lower classes, over whom the priests have
the greatest influence, on learning that the Freemasons
were excommunicated, came, naturally, to regard them
as great criminals—a feeling which it was not in the
interest of their religious instructors to remove. To
confound Protestantism with Freemasonry, was to oppose the most effectual barrier to its progress.

It is evident from these Reports that the Indians
who are Romanists by *caste* or by birth, are generally
ignorant of the difference between Romanism and Protestantism. It may appear strange that the Church of
Rome should have neglected her Indian adherents, and
taken no steps to arm them against Protestant errors.
The truth is, however, that Protestantism in Mauritius,
till within a very recent period, was of anything but an
aggressive character. It was rather the negation of
Romanism, than the assertion of any positive principle
of belief. It partook more of the character of an heir-
loom—valued no doubt, but rarely displayed to the public eye—than that of a living principle of faith lodged in
the soul, and causing its influence to be felt by all around.
The Church of Rome knew that her Indian adherents
were in no danger of being seduced into Protestant
error, so long as Protestantism existed under its previous
form in the colony ; and she therefore left them alone.
There was another cause also for this apparent indiffer-

ence.   Every Indian knows the value of money, and
has the organ of acquisitiveness largely developed.   It
is the love of money that has loosened all the ties that
bind him to his native soil, and induced him to emi-
grate to the colony.   It is the love of money that in-
duces him to remain there.   Unlike the negro, who is
content to live from hand to mouth, and has no anxiety
about the future, the Coolie has a fixed object in view,
and he is prepared to endure every privation in order
to obtain it.   He knows that it can only be obtained
by money, and that every rupee saved brings him so
much the nearer to the prize of victory.   Now, Romanism, as it exists in Mauritius, is unquestionably
an expensive religion.   It has a fixed tariff of charges
for the services it renders to a man, during all the great
events of life, from his birth to his death.   It delivers
a man from the burden of personal responsiblity, by
charging itself with the work of his salvation ; but, in
return, it expects a remuneration proportionate to
the value of the services rendered.   The negro is ever
ready to meet this demand, so far as his humble
means will permit, but the Coolie reflects twice before
parting with his money.   The sum that brings him
a step nearer to heaven, removes him further from the
goal of his earthly ambition.   The latter is close at
hand, visible and tangible, while the other is remote
and unseen ; and if the Coolie keeps all his money and
strains all his energies, in order to gratify his worldly
ambition, to the neglect of his spiritual interests, he is
perhaps not singular in his choice.   It must be borne

in mind also, that Romanism among the Coolies is merely a *caste*. It does not imply a knowledge of even the most elementary truths of the Christian faith, or the observance of any of its rites, or the partaking of any of the sacraments of the Church of Rome. Many of them, professing Romanism, have not even been baptized, and their only claim to be members of the Church of Rome rests on the fact that their fathers or forefathers had once been baptized in India. They have never been accustomed to pay for the ordinances of the religion which they profess, and the priests in Mauritius have not such a hold over their minds as to be able to persuade them to part with their money. Several of them, when admitted into the Protestant Church, expressed their joyful surprise at learning that they had nothing to pay. When Mr Taylor mentions, in his Reports, that small sums of money had been repeatedly offered to him by his Coolie hearers, he adduces the clearest proof of the acceptability of his labours, and of the effect which they produced upon the Coolie mind.

It were highly desirable that the Protestant Churches of Great Britain, that are interested in the evangelisation of India, and sending forth annually devoted missionaries to that vast field of labour, were impressed with the value of Mauritius as a missionary station, and led to perceive the important influence which it might exercise upon the success of the work which they have in view. We have already shewn that the obstacles which oppose the progress of the gospel in India, can scarcely be said to exist at all in Mauritius. Even the

Mohammedans, the most bitter opposers of Christianity in India, seem to have undergone some softening process in Mauritius. Cases of conversion have occurred among them, and they have given satisfactory proofs of their sincerity. Two of the most active and devoted colporteurs connected with the Bible Society had been followers of the false prophet. They shewed a zeal and an energy in the discharge of their duty, which placed the sincerity of their convictions beyond all question. They were consistent members of the Church of Scotland, and most regular in their attendance at her services. The questions which they put to their religious instructor often displayed a clearness of intellect and subtlety of reasoning that excited his surprise and admiration. Their journals, containing accounts of their discussions with Mohammedans, and the objections which they made to the truth of Christianity, were very interesting and highly suggestive. "God neither begets, nor is begotten," was the objection one day offered by a mollah in Malabar Town. Their reply, embodying the proofs of our Saviour's divinity, was such as might have done honour to any highly-educated Christian. The evangelisation of India will be the great question of the religious world in this country for years to come. The nation is now thoroughly in earnest upon this subject. The great error of fostering and encouraging heathenism at the expense of Christian principle is now recognised. Those even who were guided merely by feelings of expediency, feel that a different course must be adopted. The policy of Great Britain in India was to look coldly on Christianity, and to press heathenism to her heart, till, warmed by her favour, like the snake in the fable, it turned upon her and stung her. It was then felt that no cajolery, no amount of favour, no sacrifice of principle, could soften the heart or change the nature of heathenism—nay, that all such attempts impressed the native mind with the weakness of the Government which had recourse to them; and perhaps first suggested the idea of that military insurrection which has cost this country so great an expenditure of blood and treasure. The recognition of error is the first step towards amendment. There was lately presented to the world the spectacle of a great nation humbling herself beneath the mighty hand of God, and promising for the future to be guided by Christian principle in her intercourse with the natives of the Indian peninsula. She felt, and long may she continue to feel, that that vast country has been committed to her care for some nobler purpose than merely to extract its treasures or to develop its material resources; that the souls of its heathen inhabitants are a sacred deposit which God has committed to her keeping, to be answered for at a future day; and that she can only atone for past error by the strenuousness of her efforts to increase all the moral and religious influences that can have a tendency to ameliorate the spiritual condition of her heathen subjects. While the nation is in this earnest frame of mind, the importance of the influence which Mauritius may exercise upon this great work ought not to be overlooked. There are thousands of Indians who return every year from Mauritius to almost every province of their native land. They are possessed of sufficient intelligence and wealth to secure for them the respect of their poorer and more ignorant countrymen. Every one of these men might be a harbinger of the gospel, a pioneer to clear the way for the advent of the missionary, if they were only Christians. And what is to hinder them from becoming Christians? Only the apathy or the ignorance of the Churches at home, which have hitherto concentrated all their energies upon India, without producing any result adequate to the force expended. No doubt India is the chief stronghold of heathenism, where the great battle of the faith is to be fought and won, but to Christianise the Coolies of Mauritius would not be to overlook the claims of India. It would be the seizure of an outpost, from which the war could be carried into the enemy's country with every prospect of success. Moreover, the soul of a Coolie is of as much value before God as that of the highest caste Brahmin in all India, and worthy of the same care and labour. England has shewn her aristocratic tendencies even in missionary labour, by aiming at the conversion of the high-caste natives, and thus overlooking, in a great measure, the claims of their countrymen of a lower caste. A Christian Government should strike at the root of *caste*, by proclaiming and acting on the equality of all men before God. *Caste* has been the curse of India, and the greatest obstacle to missionary

efforts. England will soon be strong enough to carry
out the policy she may deem best for India, and her
first step should be to trample down caste with the
same stern determination with which she is tramp-
ling out the embers of rebellion. But *caste* has
little influence in Mauritius; it cannot cross the ocean.
The restraining power of family connexions is scarcely
felt. The Coolie stands alone, is master of his own
actions, and may become a Christian without incurring
any of that persecution to which he is exposed in India.
On his return, he is a person of some consequence
among his own relations, with whose local and foolish
prejudices he can have but little sympathy. The amount
of good which such a man might effect, if a Christian,
it would be difficult to over-estimate. The Hindoos
are, in a high degree, a social and communicative race,
fond of argument and discussion, and open to the force
of reason. Every Coolie that returns from Mauritius
a Christian would tell his heathen countrymen the
great things that God had done for him, would shew
them the Book which contains his faith, and strive to
communicate to them the knowledge of its contents.
He would thus be breaking up the soil for the missionary, and preparing it for receiving at his hands the
seeds of divine truth. While there are at this moment
about a hundred and thirty thousand Coolies of both
sexes in Mauritius, till the year 1854 little or nothing
was done to make known to them the way of salvation.
The Churches at home overlooked their spiritual re-
quirements; the few Protestant ministers in the colony,

from ignorance of their language, could do nothing. The condition of those who had been received into Christian Churches before their departure from India, was the most deplorable. They were exposed to all the temptations with-which the colony abounds, without being within the reach of any of those restraining or preventive influences which a Christian ministry can exercise. In the town of Port Louis alone, there were about a hundred of these men; and who can calculate the labour, the anxiety, the prayers that had been expended upon them by their religious instructors in India? With what joy must the accession of one convert to the Church of Christ have been hailed? And yet does it not seem strange that no steps should have been taken by any of our Protestant Churches to extend to Mauritius the ordinances of religion, and that pastoral care of which none stand in greater need than the young convert from heathenism to Christianity? Assuredly the responsibility of the missionary does not end with the profession of faith of those whom he instructs; it requires as much labour and care to keep a man in the faith as to bring him over to the faith. Considering the state of spiritual destitution to which the Indian Protestants in Mauritius were condemned, there is ground for surprise, not that some of them should have relapsed into sin, but that any of them should have continued faithful to their Christian profession. There are few, among those even who have been born within the pale of the Church, and trained from their earliest infancy in the knowledge of Christian truth, who, if exposed to the same ordeal, would

not have succumbed. This assertion is based on experience. It is to be hoped that, while measures are
being concerted for more enlarged efforts for the evangelisation of India, Mauritius will receive due consideration, not only because it presents a favourable field
for missionary labour, but also because the seeds of
divine truth sown there may be conveyed to the remot-
est provinces of India, where the foot of the missionary
has never trod. Negro preachers are always most ac-
ceptable to negroes, and native labour may yet contribute largely to the spread of divine truth in India.
There is no place where this labour may be secured with
less effort, or brought to bear with greater effect upon
India, than Mauritius. When one of Mr Taylor's
hearers declared that he had been twelve years in the
colony without having once heard that the Son of God
had come to save his soul, his words convey a bitter
reproach to those whose duty it was to have provided for
the religious instruction of his countrymen. It is to be
hoped that the time is not far distant when no Coolie
in the colony will be able to make the same assertion.

Mr Taylor's Third Report, extending to the 19th April
1855, shews an increase in the attendance at the Sunday
services, and contains proofs that the minds of the
Coolies are favourably disposed towards Christianity :—

"Having now to send you my Third Quarterly Report, I desire afresh to offer my sincere praises to the
Lord for His continued help vouchsafed to me in my
labours.

"The Sunday services, as well as the out-of-door
work, have continued to afford me as much encourage-

ment as before; and in reference to the former, you will be pleased to hear that the increasing attendance at the forenoon service having rendered it necessary to obtain a more commodious place than my house for holding it, I, with the knowledge and consent of the Mauritius Auxiliary Bible Society, applied at the end of last month to T. Y. Hugon, Esq., Protector of Immigrants, to allow me the use, on Sundays, of a large room in the Immigration Depôt. This request having been very kindly acceded to, our forenoon service has been held there since the beginning of this month, and the attendance on one occasion was thirty-seven adults, and about fifteen lads belonging to a school kept by a Romanist, besides about a dozen children belonging to the members of the congregation.

"Since my last Report, ten Bibles and fifty-eight parts of the Old Testament have been sold; and about three hundred and forty copies of the Gospels and Acts have been gratuitously distributed.

"I have also to state, that I went in the beginning of last month to Tombeau Bay, about four miles from Port Louis, and stayed there two days, distributing books, and speaking to the Tamullians in the neighbourhood. I must also mention, that as there are about a dozen Christians in that locality, who very seldom attend our Sunday services in town, and as a Christian gentleman residing there suggested the desirableness of making an effort to bring the Tamullians of that place under regular instruction, John Baptist, at the request of Mr Fenn, has gone there on three Sundays, and spoken to the Coolies in the service of Mr Milne (the gentleman above referred to), and to the Christians, who assembled in his premises. I must further state, that John Baptist has occasionally visited other places in the country, and says he has met with some encouragement among the Coolies employed by the planters and others. It will be very gratifying to the friends of the Bible Society to learn that Mr Fenn administered baptism to one of the inquirers spoken of in my last report. The convert is a peon of the Immigration Depôt, whom, together with another peon of that establishment, I, for about five months, regularly visited once a-week, with a view of preparing them for baptism. But the other individual, almost at the last moment, was deterred from receiving the rite by the opposition of his wife, who threatened to leave him. My hope, however, is, that the truths he has learned may at some future time lead him to make a bold confession of his faith in the Saviour.

" I now beg to give a few extracts from my journal:—

" '7th March 1855.—In the afternoon received a visit from M. P., a respectable Romanist, residing in Malabar Town. After he left, I went to the Immigration Depôt to instruct the two inquirers there. While reading and explaining the 18th chapter of Genesis to them, a large party of about twenty returning Coolies gathered around me, and were very much interested in the account there given of Abraham's intercession for Sodom, and of the Divine forbearance in being willing to spare that devoted city, if there should be only ten righteous persons found in it.'

"'13th March.—Addressed either groups or individuals in six different places this morning. The following remarkable incident occurred in one of these places. After I had been speaking to about a dozen persons, one of my hearers, a mule-driver, to whom I had given a book some months ago, and spoken to on four or five occasions, said to me, "Sir, read the 12th chapter to us." As he had not looked into the book I had in my hand, which was a copy of the Acts, I gave it to him to look at, and asked him whether it was in that book that he wished me to read ? He looked out for the 12th chapter, and said, " This is the chapter, sir." When I read the account of Peter's deliverance, and spoke of the care and protection exercised by the Lord over His people, my hearers seemed to be much struck ; and another of the mule-drivers said to the man above referred to, in a very earnest manner, " I often asked you on a Sunday to accompany me to the preaching-place, and you have not done so ;" to which he replied, " You know how frequently I have been unwell." '

"'16th March.—Spoke in four different places this morning. One of these places was a bazaar, the owner of which seems to be giving some attention to the Scriptures. He is mentioned two or three times before in this journal. At my request, he read the 25th and 26th chapters of the Acts to me, and as he wished to know who Paul was, I gave him an account of his life. In another place, a heathen, who first refused to receive a book, took one, after hearing me state the blessings promised to men in the Gospel. In the evening, went to Chimatomby's shop. He read the 19th chapter of the Gospel of Luke to me, and I spoke on the parable of the talents. Then addressed four men in the street, and going to another place, spoke to two others, for about ten minutes.'

" '24th March.—Spoke in four places this morning, but nothing requiring to be particularly noticed occurred. In the morning, had a very attentive congregation of Tamullians at the depôt, while engaged with the two inquirers (the peons) there. There met a heathen, who said that he had purchased a Bible from John Baptist at Pamplemoússes, and that he and another heathen had been committing the Lord's Prayer to memory, and that he had read portions from the Bible to that man, as he was not able to read, but was very anxious to embrace Christianity.'

" '25th March.—The attendance at the forenoon's service was the largest we have ever had, being forty-one adults.'

" '4th April.—Went to Malabar Town, and entering the shop of a heathen, whom I last visited on the 20th of last month, read the 23d chapter of Luke to him and the man and woman whom I there met on that occasion. They put to me a number of questions, some of them having reference to the points on which we differ from the Romanists, and said that they perceived that our mode of worship was more in accordance with the spiritual nature of God, and the dictates of reason, than that adopted by the Romanists. After conversing here for about an hour and a half, I rose to leave, when the woman said to me, "Can you not stay a little longer, sir? for by listening to these things our sins will leave us." Next went to a Romanist's shop, and spoke on the necessity of searching the Scriptures, and on the nature of the Lord's Supper. I also read part of the 11th chapter of 1st Corinthians to him. I then went into another shop kept by a heathen, who is somewhat favourably disposed toward Christianity, and spoke to five persons, including a woman. They were all very attentive, and the woman said that the Scriptures shewed "the true way of salvation." In the evening, accompanied Mr Fenn to speak to the two inquirers at the Immigration Depôt.'

"May the Lord cause His Word, which so many have heard, to run and be glorified in this colony."

Mr Taylor continued in the employment of the Madras Society till the end of June, when his engagement with them expired. His last Report to that Society was highly encouraging, and an effort was about to be made to retain his services by the local Auxiliary, when the Right Rev. Dr Ryan, the newly appointed Bishop of Mauritius, arrived in the colony. This gentleman, whose attainments as a scholar are only equalled by his humility as a Christian, and who unites the most engaging manners with devoted zeal to the cause of Christ, as soon as he arrived in the colony, began to manifest the warmest interest in all the religious Associations which he found there, and to countenance and support them in every way. His sympathy was excited when the spiritual condition of the Coolies was brought under his notice, and through his liberality Mr Taylor was enabled to continue his labours for three months longer under the direction of the Committee of the Bible Society. During this period he had an opportunity of making himself thoroughly acquainted with Mr Taylor's character, and appreciating the value of his labours among his heathen countrymen. There was only one drawback to his usefulness. Mr Fenn had returned to his own field of labour in India, and when the Coolie converts discovered that Mr Taylor could neither baptize their children, nor administer the sacrament of the Lord's Supper, their respect for him was diminished. To prevent this feeling from gaining ground among the congregation which he had organised, and which owed its existence to his labours, it was necessary that he should be admitted into sacred orders, and Dr Ryan, in the exercise of a wise discretion, ordained him to the work of the ministry. The school-house connected with the Church of England in Port Louis was set apart as a place of worship for the Coolie converts, and Mr Taylor has continued to officiate there ever since. This place, however, is not sufficiently central, and it were highly desirable that a chapel should be erected either in Malabar Town or the quarter of the Trou Fanfaron, the two spots where the Coolie population is principally located.

A passing tribute of praise is due to John Baptist, Mr Taylor's coadjutor, who, notwithstanding certain angularities of character, and a sternness of disposition similar to that of the old Covenanters, discharged his duties in such a faithful manner, as to gain the esteem of his employers, and to induce the Committee of the Bible Society to continue him in his former field of labour after the expiry of his engagement with the Madras Society. He became a consistent member of the Scotch Church, and several of the heathen baptized there owed their first knowledge of divine truth to his instructions. Towards the close of 1856, he was removed to Mahèbourg, where his wife teaches a Tamil school, while he continues to labour in connexion with the Bible Society.

After Mr Taylor's ordination and removal to the school-house as a place of worship, the Sunday service at the Immigration Depôt was not given up. Mr Taylor had devoted his attention exclusively to the Tamullians, so that the native converts from the Bengal and Bombay Presidencies, of whom there is a considerable number in the colony, derived no benefit from his services. It was considered desirable that some provision should be made for their spiritual wants. A pious officer of Engineers, whose name may yet one day be associated with those of Vicars, Lawrence, Havelock, and other Christian heroes, had formed a small missionary association, supported chiefly by the soldiers of his own corps. He raised sufficient funds to enable him to engage an intelligent Christian from the Bengal Presidency, who laboured among his countrymen partly as a Scripture-reader, and partly as a colporteur. The local Bible Society supplied him with Scriptures for sale and distribution ; but he devoted his time chiefly to reading and explaining the Word of God to his heathen countrymen, for whose benefit he opened a Sunday service at the Immigration Depôt, which was attended by about forty Bengalees.

When God has a work to be done in any land, he raises up labourers specially adapted for that work. This remark holds true of Mauritius. While the great difficulty in India, connected with the employment of native agency in evangelical labours among the heathen, appears to be the want of properly qualified men, this want has been scarcely felt in Mauritius. Devoted and Christian men, whom God seems specially to have trained for the work of imparting Christian instruction to their countrymen, came forward of their own accord and offered their services. One of these, a member of the Scotch Church, was brought under my notice under rather singular circumstances. I received a letter from the stipendiary magistrate at Port Louis, which had been addressed to him by a Coolie. It was in English, and wonderfully well written. The writer stated, that his employer had condemned him to a species of labour performed only by the lowest class of Coolies, which exposed him to the ridicule of all his countrymen, and begged the magistrate to intercede in his behalf. As he had been engaged as a house servant, I was anxious to ascertain the cause of his disgrace. It was rather ludicrous. The greatest intellectual treat of the Creole tradesman is his daily morning paper. Isaac's master had occasion to complain of the lateness of the delivery of his *Cernéen*, but his complaint brought no redress. One morning he happened to enter the kitchen, when he discovered the cause of the delay. He found Isaac conning the editorial leader, with the keenest interest painted in his countenance. He escaped with a sound beating, and the promise from his master that if he caught him again at the same offence, he would skin him alive, like a second St Bartholomew ("Il l'écorcherait tout vif, comme un autre Saint Barthélemy"). This threat deterred him for some time from a repetition of the offence. At length the craving of his mind for some intellectual food became irresistible, and he gratified his thirst for knowledge even at the risk of losing his skin. He was discovered, beaten, and degraded to do the work of a Coolie convict. I pointed out to him the impropriety of his conduct, which he fully admitted, but at the same time declared that such was the monotony of his existence, and so irresistible his craving for intellectual excitement, that he could not have avoided the reading of the only printed publication within his reach, at the risk even of undergoing the martyrdom of St Bartholomew. Assuredly this is the highest compliment that ever was paid to a Mauritius editor. More congenial labour was found for this sufferer in the cause of knowledge. After being examined as to his knowledge of Christian doctrine, and subjected to an ordeal of several months, through which he passed with an irreproachable character, he was engaged as a colporteur by the Bible Society, in whose employment he still remains.

He retained his love of knowledge, and I could always make him supremely happy by the loan of the *Home News*. This anecdote may appear trifling to some; to others it will convey a clearer insight into the Hindoo character than a whole chapter of abstract reasoning or plausible generalisation.

Another colporteur, a native of Madras, had been a pupil of the Free Church Institution, conducted by the Rev. J. Anderson, now deceased. He had received an excellent education, and spoke and wrote English with considerable ease and correctness. Though instructed in the evidences and doctrines of Christianity, and, as he himself afterwards confessed, convinced of its Divine origin as a revelation from God, a feeling of false shame prevented him from making a public confession of his faith. He remained nominally a follower of the false prophet for several years after his arrival at Mauritius ; but some of the hooked truths of God's Word had taken hold on his soul, and he could not shake them off. He would willingly have sought the advice of some Christian minister, but was employed in the interior of the island, so that he had no opportuity of consulting one. At length, God, in mercy to his soul, suffered him to be visited with a severe accident, which prevented him from leaving the hospital for several months. During his illness he made a vow, that if God restored him to health he would apply to some minister for baptism, and make a public confession of his faith in Christ. He became a communicant in the Scotch Church, and a member of my Bible class, where he gave satisfactory proofs of the excellent system of training adopted in the Free Church Institution, Madras. I relate this fact, not only because it is interesting, as shewing the workings of a mind under strong convictions of truth—it may convey encouragement perhaps to some Christian missionary who feels his heart beginning to faint and his zeal to flag, because after all his prayers and labours he sees no fruit, and no evidence that the blessing of God is with him. Let him wait with patience—his labour is not lost, it will yet bring forth fruit. "The wind bloweth where it listeth, and thou hearest the sound thereof, but canst not tell whence it cometh, and whither it goeth : so is every one that is born of the Spirit." Mr Anderson must have marked this youth's vigorous intellect ; he may have prayed for him, and watched with eagerness for some indication that his soul was moved by the power of divine truth. He watched in vain—the intellect was enlightened, but the heart was apparently untouched. God's ways are not as man's ways ; Mr Anderson died, but his work remained. The truths he had taught, by the blessing of God, exercised such a powerful influence over this man's soul that he could find no peace till he became openly a Christian. Let missionaries then take courage from the reflection which this fact naturally suggests, that though for years they may seem to have laboured in vain, and prayed in vain, their labours and prayers have not been lost—they are known to God and treasured up by Him, it may be to be reproduced at some future period, when they have gone the way of all living, with no outward memorial to mark their existence. A missionary has not lived in vain, or laboured in vain, if he has gained even one convert to Christ.

In the course of two years, about 6000 Scriptures and portions of Scripture, in the different dialects of India, were sold or distributed among the Coolies by the six colporteurs in the employment of the Auxiliary Bible Society. The good effected by this species of labour will be more evident in after years; meanwhile, there are already many pleasing proofs of the good that may be done by the reading of the Scriptures. Often when enjoying a solitary ride in the country districts during the cool part of the day, have I come upon groups of Indians, either listening with fixed attention to the reading of the Bible, or engaged in animated discussion upon some portion which had just been read. I one day examined a New Testament in Tamil, which I found an Indian reading beneath the shade of a tamarind tree in the Grande Rivière district. The margin was covered with writing, which I found to be references which he had marked for his own use— a task which he would never have undertaken if he had not felt a deep interest in the book. The following anecdote was brought under my notice by the manager of an estate in the Plaines Wilhelmes district :—The Coolies are very much addicted to gambling, and as their labours prevent them from indulging in this vice during the day, they often endeavour to practise it by stealth during the night. A good deal of irregularity of this kind had sprung up at one time upon the estate, but it was believed to have been suppressed, when the manager on one occasion returning home late at night, observed a light in a large apartment in the Indian camp. Suspecting that the Indians were gambling, he approached the window without being observed, and on looking in witnessed a sight which filled him with surprise, and perhaps gave rise to more serious feelings. A large party of Coolies were seated in a circle round one of their countrymen, who was reading by the light of a rude lamp the Word of God, to which they were listening with rapt attention. The whole scene—the reader, the audience, and the imperfect light of the lamp playing at times on their dark Oriental features—formed a subject worthy of the pencil of a Rembrandt, and produced a deep impression upon the mind of the spectator.

That the reading of the Bible by the Coolies is calculated to produce some other effect than the mere gratification of an intellectual craving, or of an idle curiosity, is proved by the fact that two congregations of Christians have arisen from the labours of the colporteurs, and that about twenty Indians were admitted into my own church, after they had given satisfactory evidence of their sincerity and of their knowledge of the doctrines of Christianity. I had no reason to regret having administered to them the ordinance of baptism; there was not a single case of apostasy amongst them; in fact, they were more exemplary and regular in their attendance at the house of God than many of those who had

been brought up as Christians. As some of them were
my own servants, I had the best opportunity of making
myself acquainted with their character and conduct;
and I can honestly testify, that I did not discover a
single case of falsehood, dishonesty, immorality, or
drunkenness amongst them, after their admission into
the Church.   On one occasion, I was absent from home
nearly two months, during which my house was left in
their entire charge, and on my return I found everything as I had left it.   I could not have done so if
they had been heathens ; they would almost to a certainty have *looted* the house and escaped with the proceeds.   My experience leads me to conclude, that the
native women are more opposed to Christianity than
their husbands, who are sometimes prevented from renouncing heathenism by their wives threatening to
leave them.   One of my servants had long been favourably disposed to Christianity, and received instruction
in its doctrines.   He was prevented from making a
profession of his faith solely by the opposition of his
wife, who, sometimes, when the subject of Christianity
was introduced, raved and stormed as if she had been
labouring under demoniacal possession.   At length a
sudden change came over her ; she expressed a desire
to be instructed in Christian doctrine ; and after a
time she and her husband were both baptized, and
married a few days afterwards.   They could not have
been actuated by any motives of self-interest ; they
knew that I intended to leave the colony soon, and that
they would have some difficulty in finding another

place. The truth is, that there is a strong antipathy among the British residents in India and Mauritius against native converts, who, it is asserted, generally retain their original evil propensities, with the acquired vices of Europeans. No doubt such cases may occur when the converts are removed from the guidance and instruction of the missionaries, at a period when they stand most in need of their counsel and aid; but there is no reason to suppose that such is the general character of this class. We have known some of them that would have reflected honour upon any Christian Church; and there is reason to fear that the British residents in India often object to native Christians as servants, because their own lives are not consistent with the principles of Christianity, and because the presence of a native convert is often felt to be a reproach to their sins.

The education of the offspring of the Coolie immigrants has hitherto been very much neglected, and they cannot be said to enjoy the same educational advantages as their parents, who have been born in India. From a calculation, grounded upon statistics collected in the colony, I am inclined to believe that about 10 per cent. of all the immigrants introduced can read and write—a proportion that may well bear comparison with the number enjoying the same advantage in England and Wales, and which forms a striking contrast with the ignorance to which their children, born in the colony, are condemned. It may be safely assumed, from the census of 1851, and the annual returns of the Protector

of Immigrants, that there are eleven thousand Indian
children of all ages up to fourteen resident in Mauritius. Of these, about five thousand eight hundred are
from four to fourteen years of age, or, in other words,
have reached that period of life when the mental faculties are sufficiently developed to profit by instruction,
and the physical frame too weak to be fit for severe or
constant toil. This remark holds particularly true in
regard to Indian children, whose mental powers soon
reach their maturity, and who shew a peculiar aptitude
for the acquisition of knowledge in early life.   No
means of instruction worthy of the name were provided
for this class till a recent period. It is true that the
Government schools are open for children of all the
races resident in the colony; but the offspring of the
Coolies, for obvious reasons, derived little advantage
from this source. These schools are taught by men
ignorant of the dialects of India, and therefore disquali-
fied for imparting instruction to children who know no
other language. The strange *patois* known as *Creole*,
which is learned by the Indian children with great
ease, is not worthy of being called a language, and can
scarcely be said to afford any facility for the acquisition
of French. Accordingly, from returns made by different
masters of the Government schools on the subject of
Indian children, it would appear that, of the five thousand eight hundred who are capable of instruction, not
more than twenty of pure Indian origin attend the Government schools, while the number of those of mixed
origin, who, while retaining their Indian names, are in

habits and associations identified with the Creole population, is about one hundred. Thus, while 10 per cent. of the Indian immigrants can read and write, only 2 per cent. of their offspring enjoy the same advantage, in a colony which almost owes its existence to the industry of their parents. It was asserted by many that the Indians did not wish their children to be educated. Although it is scarcely conceivable that men who have received the advantage of education should wish their children to be brought up in ignorance, an experiment made at the instance of the late Governor, who shewed himself on all occasions the warm friend of education, did not hold out great encouragement to those interested in this question. In 1853, a school was opened in the district of the Savanne for the instruction of Indian children, but after a period of eight or nine months, it was found that only sixteen scholars had attended, and that their progress was not at all satisfactory. This experiment was regarded by many as conclusive. It may not appear in that light, however, when the facts of the case are known. The schoolmaster, though a native of India, had no experience in education, and no interest in the subject. He accepted the place because it suited his convenience, and left it as soon as he found employment in keeping with his former habits. A school undertaken under such auspices could scarcely have succeeded, and its failure affords no indication of the state of feeling among the Coolies on the subject of education.

The ignorance in which the Indians born in the colony

are plunged, presents a serious obstacle to the success of any attempt to impart to them a knowledge of the elementary truths of religion. The most ignorant creature may, no doubt, be a recipient of Divine grace ; but it is admitted by all who are qualified to give an opinion upon this subject, that education is a most powerful auxiliary of religion, and ought not to be neglected or overlooked in any attempt at the evangelisation of the heathen. Mr Taylor, in his First Report, alludes to this subject :—" As the children of immigrants are left entirely without any education, and as many of the adults who appear anxious to have copies of the Scriptures can read but very imperfectly, the establishment of a school will be a powerful auxiliary to the object contemplated by the Bible Society. I have mentioned this verbally to the Rev. P. Beaton, Secretary of the Mauritius Auxiliary Bible Society, and at his request intend to send him a letter upon the subject."

A series of questions submitted to Mr Taylor, whose knowledge of the condition of the Indians in the colony entitles his opinions on the subject of Indian education to much weight, elicited the following replies :—

" I consider Mauritius, on the whole, as promising a field for the education of Indian children as India. The only disadvantage that seems to me to exist on the side of Mauritius, in regard to the education of the children of the Indian immigrants, is, that as even lads of ten or twelve years of age are eagerly engaged as servants, parents in indigent circumstances will be led to seek employment for their children, rather than endeavour to receive for them the benefits of education. But this disadvantage, I think, prevails no further than Port Louis, where there are so many families requiring household servants. Yet even here I am sure that no less than three purely Tamil schools, in different parts of the town, may be successfully conducted. As to the condition of Indian children here in point of education, I have only seen one regular school, kept by a Romanist, in which there are about twenty-one lads—the tuition fee of two shillings for each scholar operating as a hindrance to poor parents.

" If schools were opened, and the principles of Christianity imparted to the scholars, I do not think that any parents would object to sending their children on that account. All the schools conducted by missionaries in the Presidency of Madras, where there are so many things operating against the spread of Christianity, are conducted with the view of instilling the truths of the gospel into the minds of the rising generation. The use of heathen books of an objectionable character is strictly forbidden, and yet the heathen generally are glad to avail themselves of the gratuitous education afforded in the schools; and they have not been deterred from doing so even where conversions have repeatedly taken place, as has been the case in connexion with the English schools, conducted by the missionaries of the Free Church of Scotland, at Madras.

" I am decidedly of opinion, that as education based on Christian principles has a tendency to raise the tone of moral feeling, so must it offer a check to the com-

mission of those low and bestial crimes in which the
poor ignorant heathen, whose minds are under the con-
taminating influence of a corrupt religion, often delight
to indulge.   The education imparted in vernacular
mission schools in India is of the simplest kind, embracing no more than elementary studies ; but where
the object is to reach the higher class of Hindoos,
English is always taught.   In these schools, the standard of education varies considerably.   Masters for the
vernacular schools may be had in the colony at an
average of twelve dollars per month, allowing about
six dollars per month for house-rent, and fourteen
dollars per month for school-books. The annual cost of
each vernacular school, including contingencies, would
be about 230 dollars (£46) per annum."

   There are few among the labouring classes in England
who would be willing to pay a school-fee of two shillings
per month for each of their children, and yet the worst
paid agricultural labourers in England gain twice as
much money in the shape of wages as the Coolies in
Mauritius. When a Coolie pays two shillings per month
for the education of one of his children, he is expending
one-eighth of his whole income on that child ; and the
fact that there are parents amongst them prepared to
make this sacrifice, affords the strongest proof of their
desire to procure for their offspring the same educational advantages which they themselves enjoyed in
India. I visited the school taught by the Romanist. It
was situated in a miserable lane, in the neighbourhood
of the Trou Fanfaron.   Delicacy and a sense of pro-

priety prevent me from entering into details ; suffice it to say that the slums of Westminster are clean and healthy compared with the hotbeds of cholera and fever, in this quarter, that remain unvisited by the police and uncared for by the Municipality. There was no window, or means of ventilating the horrid little den, where about twenty Indian boys were assembled, and half suffocated by the foul atmosphere which they breathed. How a school could have been conducted in such a place, without the scholars having been decimated by fever, seems inexplicable. And yet, in 1855, this was the only school for the education of the thousands of Indian children that swarm in the streets of Port Louis. The Government, after the failure of the school at the Savanne, did nothing further in the matter, and before they would resume consideration of the question, it was necessary to prove by experiment that the education of the Indian children was practicable. Through the kind assistance of General Hay, Messrs Stein and Campbell, and a few other members of my congregation, I was enabled to open an Indian school in a healthy part of the town, where the population consisted principally of Coolies. Its success proved that the Indian parents are, at least in many instances, anxious to secure the education of their children. The average attendance was about ninety children of both sexes, although the boys preponderated. School-books were procured from Madras, and the progress made by the pupils was very great. Instruction wa. imparted in Tamil, the only language with which they were acquainted. Their ignorance of English or French prevented them from deriving any advantage from the Government schools, the teachers of which are ignorant of the dialects of India, the only medium through which instruction can be conveyed to them.

The success of this experiment was brought under the attention of the local Government, and the question of Indian education opened up afresh. The cause found a warm advocate in the newly appointed Attorney-general, Mr Dickson ; and in 1857, an ordinance was passed rendering the education of children of a certain age compulsory. The utility of this measure will depend very much upon the spirit in which it is carried out. No assistance can be expected from the Creole planters, who as a class are opposed to the education of the lower orders, and unless the Government be firm, this ordinance, like many others, may remain a dead letter. So far as the Indian children are concerned, any attempt to impart instruction to them save through the medium of their mother tongue must prove a failure. When the Vicar of Wakefield's son undertook to teach the Dutch English, he forgot that to do so he must first learn Dutch himself. Government-school teachers undertaking the task of Indian education, find themselves exactly in the same predicament. It ought not to be forgotten, moreover, that Mauritius is a British colony, and if the knowledge of any foreign language is to be imparted to them, the preference ought to be given to English, and not to

French, which can be of no use to those amongst them who return to India. There can be no difficulty in procuring from India teachers familiar both with English and with the different dialects of their native country, and these are the only men who can be useful as teachers among the Coolie children. Above all, they ought to be sound Protestants and consistent Christians. England has kept good faith with the inhabitants of Mauritius. She has not only preserved the established religion, as she was bound to do by the terms of capitulation—she has done much to strengthen and promote it. Let her shew herself for once to be Protestant and consistent, by insisting that the principles of that faith which she herself professes, and of none other, shall be taught in the Indian schools. This will be only just. The Church of Rome has done nothing for the Coolies in Mauritius ; she has practically ignored their existence. The Protestant Churches have taken the initiative in this matter, they have been the first to occupy the field, and our earnest prayer is that they may be able to retain it, and that Mauritius may yet be the Icolmkill of India—the small but central point from which the rays of divine truth shall emerge to aid in dispersing the clouds of heathen ignorance that are still impending over that vast peninsula.

CHAPTER VII.

FROM the pictures of social life in Mauritius already
presented to the view, no sanguine expectation could
be entertained that education and religion, the two
greatest humanising and elevating influences that can
be brought to bear upon any community, are in a
satisfactory condition. In colonial life, as in all primitive states of society, the attention of men is first
directed to the means of satisfying the more immediate wants of nature, which are far more urgent than
the cravings of the intellect and the soul for mental
and spiritual food. In slave colonies the wants of our

spiritual nature are generally overlooked, and, in truth, the system of slavery is so degrading and brutalising, that its victims soon lose all capacity for receiving secular or religious instruction. Those also who profit by that system are, from motives of self-interest, opposed to the spread of education among the slaves, which could only render them dissatisfied with their condition and increase their thirst for liberty. The planter of Mauritius, who, after working his slave through the day, sent him out to hunt for his food in the forests at night, was not at all likely to feel a deep interest in his education. The only schoolmaster he knew was the commandant, the only discipline the driver's whip. The *animus* prevalent in the colony with regard to the education of the lower classes appears from an ordinance on public instruction, passed by the local legislature in 1835, which requires teachers of private schools to obtain the previous sanction of Government; and, even when obtained, it might be withdrawn on report of the Committee of Instruction, which consisted of thirteen members chosen by the local Government. By the same ordinance it was enacted, that any party opening a school without permission was liable to a fine not exceeding £20 sterling, and to have his school closed.* The object of this ordinance is obvious. The Committee of Instruction was composed of men resolutely opposed to the education of the lower classes, and they were thus invested with a power which enabled them

* It was afterwards rejected by the Home Government.

to frustrate every attempt made by missionaries or others to open schools for imparting the elements of secular and religious knowledge to the negroes.

In truth, the planters of Mauritius, till the close of the last century, seem to have received little education themselves, and must have regarded any attempt to educate their slaves as little better than a *mauvaise plaisanterie*. One can conceive one of these worthies, on hearing the question of popular education first broached by an enthusiastic young missionary, addressing him in language similar to that of the Principal of Louvain—"You see me, young man; I never had any education, and I don't find that I ever missed it. I have been made a member of the Committee of Instruction without education; I have ten thousand dollars a-year without education; I eat my curry heartily without education; and, in short, as I have no education, I do not believe there is any good in it." The advantages of education were not publicly recognised till the foundation of the Royal College in 1791; and even then they were confined to one small section of the community. I never met with an old slave who could read or write, and when the British and Foreign Bible Society offered a Testament after the abolition of slavery to every one of the apprentices who could read, it was found that out of a negro population of about 70,000 souls, there were only ten who could profit by the gift. It is only rendering an act of justice to former British slaveholders to state, that in the West Indies there were 100,000 applicants for the same gift.

In glancing at the state of education, at the present moment, it may be well to calculate the number of those who are old enough to receive instruction, and to contrast it with the number actually attending educational establishments. In making this calculation, no account is taken of the offspring of Indian parents resident in the colony. Their position in regard to education is considered in another part of this work.

From a Report of a Special Committee of Council, dated 7th February 1855, it appears that education had made little progress among the lower classes of society. According to the returns of the census made in 1851, there were about 38,000 Creole children of all classes (excluding Indian) in the colony. Of these 23,500 were between the ages of four and fourteen, or at that period of life when the opportunities of imparting instruction are most available, and the mind's receptivity most active.

From the Report of the Superintendent of Government schools for the year 1854, it appears that the total number of children (of whatever origin) attending these schools was 2089, or deducting the Indian children, of whom very few attend, that the Creole pupils amounted to 2000. If a small allowance be made for the increase in the juvenile Creole population between 1851 and 1855, it may be calculated that the proportion then borne by the scholars attending the Government schools, to the juvenile population between four and fourteen years of age, was 8·5 per cent.

But education is not confined to the Government schools, though they alone bring the elements of useful knowledge within the reach of the lower classes of the community. There is the Royal College, and several private schools, in Port Louis, besides those in connexion with the Church of Rome, and the Society for the Propagation of Christian Knowledge. The number of pupils attending these different institutions in 1855, was calculated at 3500. If to this number be added the 2000 attending the Government schools, it will follow that the proportion of Creole children receiving instruction to the whole juvenile population is about 14 per cent., or 22 per cent. to the 23,500 between the ages of four and fourteen.

In 1857, the pupils attending the different schools in the colony were 5376, viz. :—

Attending Royal College,	. . .	284
,,	Government Schools, . .	1860
,,	Christian Knowledge Society's Schools,	89
,,	Private Schools, . .	2235
,,	Roman Catholic Schools, .	908
		5376

The scholars of the different schools amounted in 1855 to 5500, exclusive of Indian children, while in 1857, including all classes, they amounted only to 5376. As there must have been a considerable increase in the juvenile population in the course of two years, this result shews that education is rather retrograding than advancing in Mauritius, and that the proportion of educated to non-educated children is even less than

14 per cent. The proportion of the whole population that can read and write to those who do not possess this advantage is about 8 per cent. In this estimate no account is taken of the Indian population. The Coolie immigrants are, on the whole, a better educated class than the Creoles.

According to the last census of England and Wales (excluding other parts of the British Empire), out of a juvenile population of more than four millions of children, between the ages of five and fifteen, 1,768,000 were attending day schools, so that the proportion of the educated to the non-educated was more than 44 per cent., and the proportion of day scholars to the whole population about 10 per cent. It follows from this that there are 2 per cent. more of day scholars in England than of persons of all ages in Mauritius that can read and write.

The whole extent of the ignorance prevalent among the lower classes in the colony, is not brought to light by this calculation. Their children form a very small part of the 14 per cent. that are receiving instruction. While in England nearly nine-tenths of the whole instruction given by national, denominational, public, and parochial schools is, by its very nature, designed for the benefit of those who will have to earn their bread by the sweat of their brow, in Mauritius more than 30 per cent. of the whole instruction given is devoted to those whose prospects in life elevate them above the conditions of manual labour. While only about 14 per cent. of the whole juvenile population are receiving the advantages of education, an unusually

large proportion of this fraction are enjoying an education such as wealth or easy circumstances alone can
procure.   Out of about 25,000 children, the number
at which those between four and fourteen years of age
in 1857 may be estimated, only 5376, including Indian
children, were receiving any kind of instruction, and at
least one-third of these were receiving an education
such as comparatively wealthy parents alone can supply,
and the remaining two-thirds a lower kind, while some
20,000 Creole children, old enough to receive instruction, were left in a state of utter ignorance.   If to these
20,000 Creole children be added about 6000 Coolie
children of the same age, the whole number of children
capable of receiving instruction and condemned to
ignorance, in 1857, was about 26,000.   The evils resulting from the gross ignorance of the lower classes
in Mauritius cannot be over-estimated.   It places them
beyond the pale of civilisation, and renders the labours
of the missionary of little use.   When youth has been
spent in ignorance and vice, instead of being devoted
to self-improvement and the acquisition of knowledge,
the whole nature of a man becomes so degraded that
he cannot comprehend the truths of revelation, or receive them for his guidance.   No doubt the Spirit of
God can act anywhere, and wherever He acts, He acts
irresistibly, so as to quicken those who are spiritually
dead ; but it is not necessary at the present day to prove
that education and the gospel, the schoolmaster and the
missionary, should go hand in hand, and that when
their labours ·are separated, humanly speaking, little

success can be expected. At the present day, Protestant ministers find access to the Creole population only through the Bible, and to those who cannot read the Bible is a sealed book.

The Royal College, founded soon after the outbreak of the French Revolution, has conferred many advantages upon the children of the upper classes, and its French rectors appear to have been men of a superior class. Many of its pupils have distinguished themselves in Europe, and the education imparted is equal to that of the public schools in England. The religious element has been excluded, in order to conciliate the Roman Catholic part of the population. As might have been expected, this sacrifice of principle was unsuccessful in securing the end in view, and in 1852 the Roman Catholic bishop opened a rival college, which, after dragging out a comatose existence of a few months, expired. The Creole parents shewed that they esteemed a sound education without the religious element, a greater boon than an imperfect education according to the strictest principles of Romanism.

The success of the Royal College, as of every similar institution, must depend in a great measure upon the character and acquirements of the rector and his staff of assistants. At one period, when under the direction of a French rector, the pupils amounted to four hundred, but in 1845 there were only one hundred and eighty. It will be already observed that the present number is considerably larger, and yet the college might attract a far larger attendance.

Mr Meldrum, one of the professors, has received the advantages of a university education, and while highly successful in imparting a knowledge of mathematics to his pupils, has been able to devote much of his time to the study of meteorological science, for the cultivation of which Mauritius affords many facilities.   One great means of enhancing the usefulness of the Royal College, and of attracting a higher class of teachers, would be to make the salary of each professor equal to that of a colonial chaplain, and to bestow such appointments only upon those who are graduates of universities. So long as the professors are under-paid, it cannot be expected that a high class of men will expose themselves to exile, and to all the inconveniences of Mauritius life, for the sake of the miserable pittance which the Government allows in the shape of salary to the professors.   Under the present system, these men have no recognised status in society, apart from that which their individual talents or acquirements may procure for them, and no adequate retiring allowance, after their energies are exhausted by the labours of their arduous profession. A grant of £1000 per annum, to supplement the salaries of the professors, would do much to procure a higher class of men for these appointments, and to raise the Royal College to a degree of efficiency to which it has never attained under the present system.

The private schools in Port Louis do not deserve any special notice.   The education imparted in them is adapted to children, whose tender years prevent them from attending the Royal College, or to those whose parents are opposed to the use of the English language, the medium of instruction in that institution. The decrease in the number of pupils attending the Royal College is ascribed, in some measure, to the establishment of these schools.

Lady Mico's Charity, the object of which was to extend the advantages of religious and moral instruction to the negroes and coloured population of the British colonies, included Mauritius within the field of its useful labours. A large proportion of the limited number of those who can read and write among the negro and coloured population, are indebted for this advantage to the schools in connexion with Lady Mico's Charity. These schools have been given up, and the Government schools, founded on a different basis, and supported by the colony, have been erected in their stead. The exclusion of all religious instruction is one of the rules most stringently enforced in these schools. The teachers are permitted to read a portion of Scripture in the morning, but they are prohibited from explaining, or making any remarks upon the portion they read. At one time, an order was issued from the Colonial Secretary's office, prohibiting the reading of the Scriptures, but it was immediately suppressed. The object of this restriction, in regard to the explanation of the Scriptures, is to avoid exciting the prejudices or fears of the Roman Catholic priests and parents; and this attempt to secure their good-will, by the sacrifice of Protestant principle, has been about as successful as the endeavour to secure the loyalty of the Brahmins in

India by ignoring Christianity. So long as the teachers in these schools are Protestants, the priests cannot but regard them with distrust, and look upon the restriction about the explanation of the Scriptures as only a blind to conceal the proselytising spirit by which they are actuated. The priests, therefore, on this ground, are opposed to these Government schools, and have dissuaded their adherents from allowing their children to attend them. They could not well do this, without providing other schools, under their own direction, where the children could be instructed without the danger of imbibing Protestant error. Accordingly, they have done so in some of the country districts, and their influence, in one or two cases, has had the effect of nearly emptying the Government schools. As a general rule, the Church of Rome is not favourable to education. The blind credulity which she demands from her adherents can only flourish in the soil of ignorance; but, Proteus-like, she can change her outward form according to circumstances, and appear as the advocate or the enemy of education, just as it may suit her interests. She holds the coloured population of Mauritius too firmly in her grasp to dread the relaxing effect of a small dose of education administered by her own priests.

If Mauritius is ever to rank among the civilised dependencies of the British crown, and to enjoy that self-government which is being gradually extended to other British colonies, effectual steps must be taken for the removal of that ignorance, to which more than four-fifths of her inhabitants are at present condemned. It is sufficiently clear, from the statistics already given, that the present educational machinery is altogether insufficient for the supply of the wants of the community, and that education itself, before its blessings can be extended to the lower classes, must be placed upon a different basis. In highly-educated communities, where the advantages of knowledge are felt and recognised by all, interference on the part of the State may be unnecessary, because every parent, having experienced in his own case the advantages of education, will strive to procure the same blessing for his children ; but in Mauritius, where the mass of the people are sunk in the most deplorable ignorance, and careless of everything save the gratification of their immediate wants, it is the duty of the State to intervene, and to rescue the rising generation from the ignorance in which their parents are plunged. Selfishness is the characteristic of colonial life, and it would be vain to look in Mauritius for the establishment of any of those institutions for the education of the lower classes, to which Christianity has given birth in England and elsewhere. Nothing is to be expected from private generosity, or charitable feeling, or ecclesiastical munificence. If the lower classes are ever to be educated, the work must be undertaken, carried on, and completed by the State. It is as absurd to expect these classes to educate themselves, as to expect a dead man to restore himself to life ; the principle of vitality is equally wanting in both cases. The objection, that education will unfit its recipients for the duties of their humble position, has no force when applied to those who have no knowledge of, or regard for these duties—who contribute nothing to the general prosperity—who in ordinary times live from hand to mouth on the unearned produce of a prodigal soil—and who in times of famine or want fall back upon that provision which the law has made for their subsistence, at the expense of the industry of the working part of the community.

In the neighbouring island of Bourbon, after the recent abolition of slavery, the Government, in order to prevent the emancipated slave population from abusing their liberty, and training up their children in indolence, ignorance, and vice, established *atéliers d'industrie* in connexion with the schools that were opened. The object of these work-shops was to teach a useful trade to the children of the former slaves, and thus enable them to occupy a respectable and useful place in society. A similar system, conjoining the work-shop with the school, and making attendance at both compulsory, might be highly beneficial in Mauritius. It would be only an extension of the principle already adopted in England, by the establishment of schools in connexion with factories, with this difference, that there would be small factories in connexion with the schools. Besides the mechanical arts, many branches of industry might be cultivated in these schools, and an impetus thus given to the development of the material resources of the island hitherto unknown. At present, sugar is the staple article of produce, and if the cane should become subject to disease, so as to fail in yielding the ordinary supply, the whole community, dependent for its support on this single resource, would be exposed to want and misery. The instruction of the lower classes in the cultivation of other branches of industry, would serve in some measure as an antidote against the occurrence of this evil.

The expectation that the descendants of the slave population in Mauritius will ever hire themselves out as agricultural labourers, so as to supersede the necessity for the present supply of labour from India, or that the diffusion of education among them will alter their feelings on this subject, will never be realised. The remembrance of the horrors of slavery is engraven upon their memories with a pen of iron, and no lapse of time will ever erase it. Labour in the fields will ever be regarded by them as a mark of degradation, on account of the painful associations and memories which it awakens. It is different with other kinds of manual labour. The Creoles exhibit considerable skill in acquiring a knowledge of the mechanical arts, but, from want of instruction, every kind of skilled labour is very rare and expensive. The establishment of work-shops, under the care of skilful mechanics, similar in character to those now occasionally employed as lay missionaries in India, would be productive of much good, and prevent a large portion of the population from becoming dependent, at any period of unusual pressure, upon the general resources of the colony, to the formation or increase of which they have in no way contributed.

In 1857, after considerable opposition, an ordinance was passed by the Legislative Council, by which education was rendered compulsory on all classes in Mauritius. If this law is not to remain, like many others, a dead letter in the statute-book, it will be necessary that the sum previously voted annually for education, amounting to nearly £11,000, be doubled, so as to defray the expense of the additional Government schools that must be opened. As no law can be executed unless it carry with it the approval of the community whom it affects, and as the planters are generally opposed to the education of the lower classes, unless the local Government shew more than their usual firmness, this attempt may prove a failure, and the reign of ignorance and vice may be perpetuated. To render the attempt successful, it will be necessary to secure the services of more efficient teachers than are to be found at present in the Government schools. These schools are, at present, the last refuge of the destitute, and the social position assigned to the teachers, though equal perhaps, in most cases, to their merits, is such as to hold out no inducement to any man of education to accept such an appointment. They have nothing to aspire to beyond the pittance doled out to them as a retiring allowance, when they are no longer fit for service. They have no personal interest in the success of their schools; they receive the same pay for ten scholars as for one hundred, and thus they are under the influence of none of those feelings or motives that, in other professions, excite men to exertion. Every pupil at a Government school pays one shilling per month as a fee, but the teacher has no share in this sum, which is collected for the Government. If the salaries of the teachers were partly dependent upon the number of their pupils, there would be a larger attendance at the schools. A man who really loves his profession, and is guided by a high sense of duty, will not be influenced by such considerations; and Mr Clerk's school at Mahèbourg, both as regards attendance and the intelligence of the pupils, is an evidence of the large amount of good that one such man can effect. Such cases, however, are exceptional, and the establishment of additional schools, or the enforcement of attendance, will produce little benefit, unless the services of a higher class of teachers be secured. The whole question of education in Mauritius is worthy of the attention and revisal of the Home Government.

Romanism is the form of religion to which the vast majority of the Creole population are nominally attached. The few husbandmen from Bourbon who first settled in the island, after its desertion by the Dutch, yielded the management of their temporal and spiritual affairs to a few missionaries of the order of St Lazarus, who exercised the same influence over their minds as the parish *curés* among the simple-minded peasantry of France at the present day. The island, however, was soon overrun by adventurers of all classes from France, who openly avowed the infidel principles of the Encyclopædists, and lived in the open neglect of all the ordinances of religion. The seeds of infidelity thus sown in the Mauritius soil have taken deep root, and produced their natural fruit in the irreligion and immorality that pervade all classes of the community. The influence of the priests has not been able to stem the tide of infidelity, and the principles of Voltaire have more influence than those of Jesus Christ. The lower orders have adopted the outward form of Christianity, without being instructed in its doctrines or imbued with its spirit, and Mauritius occupies the invidious distinction of being the most irreligious of all our British colonies.

When the island was captured by the British in 1810, it was stipulated by the terms of capitulation that the established religion should be preserved. If the British Government had confined themselves to the strict terms of this agreement, the support of the Roman Catholic clergy would not have been a heavy burden on the Colonial Treasury. In 1810, the population of Mauritius amounted to about 80,000, and there were only four priests to watch over the spiritual interests of all the inhabitants. These priests were paid on the strictest principles of economy, £100 being the annual salary of each; so that the whole ecclesiastical establishment of the colony cost only £400 per annum, about one half of the sum which is now paid annually as salary to the Roman Catholic Bishop. As each priest had the cure of 20,000 souls, little or no effort seems to have been made to instruct the slave population in the principles of religion. A few of them may have been baptized, but the cruel treatment to which they were daily subjected must have prejudiced them against the religion of their masters. The promise of heaven in a future world could have but little attraction for them if that heaven was to be the home of their tormentors on earth. They were shrewd enough to suspect that the white men would gain the supremacy over them there, and found more comfort in the belief that, after death, they would be restored to their kindred and their native land. The British Government have done everything in their power to increase the influence of the Church of Rome. Instead of preserving the established religion on the basis on which they found it, or increasing the number of priests in proportion to the increase in the population, they have nearly quadrupled the number of priests, and pay to the Roman Catholic Bishop annually about twice as much as the French paid to their whole ecclesiastical establishment. The 80,000 inhabitants of the colony in 1810 were nominally attached to the Church of Rome, because no other religion was recognised by the State. The present nominal adherents of the Church of Rome do certainly not exceed that number, and their knowledge of her tenets is perhaps not much greater than in 1810, and yet there are now in Mauritius thirteen priests, who receive from the Colonial Treasury an average salary of £200 each, and a Roman Catholic Bishop, who receives £780. The established religion has certainly been preserved, and something more.

The Government were not satisfied with increasing the number and doubling the pay of the priests of the

Church of Rome; they countenanced her idolatrous rites, by commanding Protestant officers and soldiers to be present at, and to take part in them. At the great annual festival of that Church, the *fête de Dieu,* which was celebrated with much pomp, the most beautiful girls in the colony walked in procession through the streets in white robes and with uncovered heads, strewing flowers before the "Host," and the streets through which the procession passed were lined by British soldiers, who presented arms and fired salutes in honour of what all Protestants must regard as an act of gross idolatry. I have met with many Christian men in the ranks of the British army, and if one of these had refused to take part in this idolatrous rite, his refusal would have cost him his life. This blot on the escutcheon of Protestant England has now been removed by the noble stand made by a pious officer of artillery, who sacrificed his future prospects in life in order to do away with this reproach to his religion and his country.* The salutes are now fired by the cannon at the Roman Catholic Bishop's palace, the finest building in the colony.

At the capture of the island there were only two Roman Catholic churches in the colony, one at Port Louis and the other at Pamplemousses. At the present moment the whole island is studded with chapels, some of which have been erected by a tax levied on Protestants and Roman Catholics without distinction.

* A similar incident, attended with the same result, occurred at Malta.

The churches at Mahèbourg, Plaines Wilhelmes, and Poudre d'Or are very handsome buildings. Wherever a few negro huts are huddled together, one of them is erected into a chapel, which differs from the others only by the cross erected at one of its extremities. Occasional services are held there, and no effort is spared by the priests, under the guidance of Dr Collier their Bishop, to bring the black and coloured population within the pale of their Church. Any religion, however imperfect, must be preferable to the utter irreligion, ignorance, and vice in which these classes were plunged before the abolition of slavery. At that period, so powerful were the feelings of gratitude which the negro and coloured population entertained towards their benefactors, that having no religion, they were prepared to receive any form that Great Britain might have offered them; but no effort was made, the golden opportunity passed by never to return, and they accepted rather than chose Romanism, as the only form of religion within their reach. Many of the negroes are still strongly attached to their ancient superstitions. and have no connexion with the Church of Rome beyond an occasional attendance at her gorgeous ceremonies, which are calculated to make a profound impression on the African mind. The priests endeavour to gain their observance of the outward forms of religion, without instructing their minds in the doctrines of that religion which they profess. A few miracles are said to have been attempted; but they do not appear to have had a great success. In short, the

mass of the Mauritius population of Creole origin,
while nominally Christian, are ignorant of the most
elementary truths of Christianity, and regard their
priests either with slavish fear or superstitious reve-
rence. Many facts might be adduced in proof of this
assertion ; one may suffice. When the present Roman
Catholic Bishop arrived in the colony, some years ago,
after a visit to Europe, the lower classes turned out in
large numbers to witness his landing. The streets
resounded with the acclamation, "Monseigneur fin
venè," and the rejoicing was unbounded. A quiet
merchant, passing through the crowd, inquired at a
Creole woman, who was using her lungs lustily, who it
was that had come? Looking at him with mingled
surprise and contempt, she answered, "Comment donc !
vous n'a pas connè? Monseigneur Jesu Christ fin
venè."*

The present Roman Catholic Bishop has done much
in Mauritius for the Church to which he belongs. He
found her despised, and he has caused her to be feared,
if not respected. By his own confession, he would have
preferred the military to every other profession, but as
circumstances have forced on him the crosier instead
of the sword, he has indulged his warlike temperament
by commencing a crusade against Freemasonry, the
rival institution of Romanism in the colony. He denounced Freemasonry in one of his charges, as forming
one of those secret societies against which a Papal bull
had been directed, and proceeded to excommunicate all

* "What, you not know ? My Lord Jesus Christ is come."

the Freemasons who proved *récalcitrant.* Though this
measure exposed him to the abuse of a licentious press,
and created much unhappiness in many private families,
he adhered to it with a firmness worthy of a Hildebrand,
and carried it against all opposition. He possesses the
highly polished manners and insinuating address by
which many of the higher dignitaries of the Church of
Rome are distinguished, and in matters of diplomacy
connected with his own Church has proved himself
more than a match for the simple-minded Governors
with whom he has had to deal. If, in extending the
influence of his Church, he has looked more to the accession of numbers than to the diffusion of religious
instruction, and been satisfied with an external observance of the rites of religion, without demanding a
knowledge of those truths of which these rites are
symbolical, the fault rests less with him as an individual
than with the system which he represents. However
imperfect the teaching of the Church of Rome in Mauritius may be, she has done more for the Creole population than the Church of England, which had previously
kept herself aloof from them, and has only of late years
begun to bestir herself in their behalf, when little hope
of success can be entertained.

After the capture of the island, a civil and a military
chaplain were appointed to labour among the members
of the Church of England, resident or stationed in the
colony. Tradition has failed to preserve the name of
the military chaplain, while his brother of the civil
service seems to have been a man of the Trulliber cast,

whose sole claims to posthumous fame rest on the fact, that he grew the largest cabbages and produced the best butter of any man in the colony. Neither of these men did much to strengthen the stakes or to enlarge the cords of the Church to which they belonged. Two civil chaplains were afterwards appointed, and one of them, the Rev. Mr Banks, took a warm interest in the spiritual welfare of the Creole population, and formed a small congregation of ex-apprentices, while stationed at Plaines Wilhelmes. The peculiar circumstances in which he was placed prevented him from entering upon, or carrying into execution, those schemes for the moral elevation of the lower classes which he had so much at heart, and being left for many years without co-operation or sympathy, he might have said with Elijah, " I, even I only, remain a prophet of the Lord." He was mainly instrumental in raising the funds for the erection of the neat little chapel at Plaines Wilhelmes, where he officiated for some time, and if his valuable life had been spared, his future career, free from every obstacle, might have been one of great usefulness. Good men are often removed while they seem to be most needed on earth, while the useless, like unripe fruit, are passed by.

Mr Banks found an assistant in his labours among the Creoles, in a young medical officer on the staff, stationed at Bambou. Touched by the spiritual " darkness visible" of the Creoles who came to consult him about their bodily diseases, he began to speak to them of that still greater disease of the soul, for which the

Great Physician alone has provided a remedy. He who alone can give efficacy to such labours, verified His own promise, " My word shall not return unto me void." There was a shaking among the dry bones of heathenism, and some of those who had been recently emancipated from the chains of slavery by the generosity of Great Britain, were by the grace of God emancipated from the still more grievous slavery of sin. The little church thus formed at Bambou became as a light shining in a dark place, the rays of which found entrance elsewhere.

Through the liberality of Lady Gomm, a small chapel was erected near Réduit, the Governor's country residence, for affording the means of worship to those resident in the Moka district, who, owing to the distance, could not attend church in Port Louis. As there has been no resident clergyman either at Moka or at Plaines Wilhelmes, Protestantism has not taken root among the Creole inhabitants of either of these districts, and the small Creole congregation formed by Mr Banks at Plaines Wilhelmes dwindled away after his removal to Port Louis.

In 1850, the colony received a visit from Dr Chapman, the Bishop of Ceylon. As he was the first Protestant Bishop who had ever touched its soil, many Episcopalians, who were well advanced in years, profited by his visit and were confirmed. While it is questionable whether the incorporation of Mauritius with the diocese of Ceylon would have been an advantage to the former, there can be no doubt but that Dr Chapman's visit roused the Protestants from the spiritual lethargy into which they had sunk, and gave an impetus to Protestant principles, the effect of which is still felt. Under his auspices the Mauritius Church Association was formed, the object of which is to propagate the doctrines of the Church of England in the colony. This Association engaged and paid a missionary, the Rev. Gideon de Jeux, who laboured under their direction in the districts of Plaines Wilhelmes and Black River for three years, at the end of which he was placed on the staff of colonial chaplains, and paid by the Government. The congregation formed by the medical officer at Bambou is under the care of Mr de Jeux, whose labours extend over a large extent of country. The spiritual destitution under which the former slave population and their descendants are labouring may be learned from the fact, that in 1853 he baptized 174 adults, who had been living in a state of heathenism. It appears that Mr de Jeux's usefulness is much enhanced by his knowledge of the healing art, and that his skill as a physician is only equalled by his success as a missionary.

The Seychelle group of islands is a dependency of Mauritius, and the residence of a Civil Commissary. Until 1832 there was no minister of any Christian Church stationed in these islands, and the inhabitants lived, died, and were buried without the benefit of any religious ordinances. In 1832, a minister of the Church of England was appointed to the Seychelles; but after one year's experience he quitted the colony, which was afterwards visited by the Rev. Mr Banks. The religious services which he conducted were well attended, and he baptized and married a great many that had never been admitted into any Church, and had only been married by the Civil Commissary. Having been authorised by about four thousand of the inhabitants to represent their spiritual destitution to the Government, and if possible to secure the services of a minister of the Church of England, he was successful in his efforts in their behalf, and Mr Delafontaine, a native of Switzerland, was appointed Civil Chaplain at Seychelles. In 1855, this gentleman was succeeded by the Rev. Dr Fallait, whose knowledge of the French language and superior attainments give promise of much usefulness in his remote and isolated field of labour. In 1853, the Council of Government extended the Church Building Ordinance, already in force in Mauritius, to the Seychelles Islands, and there is reason to believe that a building devoted to the exclusive service of God has now been erected in these distant dependencies.

Dr Ryan, the present Bishop of Mauritius, arrived in the colony in June 1855. His appointment has been a most fortunate one, and it were highly desirable, for the sake of sound religion and of peace, that men of similar principles were appointed to the Episcopate in other British colonies. From the moment of his arrival he manifested that catholic spirit, and ready co-operation in every good work, that have procured for him the confidence and esteem of all sections of the Protestant community, and led him to be regarded as the model of a missionary Bishop. Many after leaving the colony will look back to their intercourse with him with feelings of unmingled pleasure, and unite their sincere prayers that the blessing of Almighty God may rest upon the labours of His accomplished and devoted servant. Since his arrival two new churches have been opened at Mahè-bourg and Pamplemousses, and also a Seamen's Float-ing Chapel in the harbour of Port Louis, where the Rev. Mr Bichard, who devotes his whole time to the seamen, officiates. Through Dr Ryan's influence and efforts the number of Protestant ministers has been increased.

No sketch of the condition of religion in Mauritius would be complete without a brief allusion to the labours of the venerable John Le Brun, who has been labouring as a missionary in the colony, under the direction of the London Missionary Society, for nearly forty years. The good old man ! I think I see him still, with his snow-white hair, his open honest coun-tenance, his simple but touching eloquence, and his earnest faith—an Israelite indeed, in whom there is no guile. He might have sat as the original of the Swiss pastor, La Roche, in Mackenzie's beautiful tale. For a period of nearly forty years he has continued to labour among the negro and coloured population, and the history of his labours would be highly interesting. He has had to surmount many difficulties, and to struggle against many disadvantages ; but his earnest, buoyant faith has never forsaken him. I have heard him relate, with a *naïveté* that lent additional charms to the narrative, the account of the failure of his first attempt to form a congregation in Port Louis. There was a strong prejudice against him and his mission, and though he hired a room, none would attend. He was sneered at as a Methodist, and everything done by the petty local authorities to annoy and discourage him. At length he saw that if any good was to be done among the coloured people he must go out to the highways, and force them to come in. He commenced the experiment with four young *gamins*, whom he found playing in the street. He enticed them into his little chapel, and engaged in prayer. Feeling that his work was now really begun, he was most earnest in imploring a blessing upon it. At length he concluded, and was proceeding to address his audience, when to his surprise he found himself alone. The audience had disappeared during the prayer. This failure, however, did not discourage him ; other attempts were made, and accompanied with better success. The jealousy of the police was excited, and his meetings were suppressed by the application of a local law, still in force, which forbids more than fifteen persons to assemble in one place without the permission of the Governor. At length he obtained immunity from this absurd restriction, and has ever since continued to enjoy that religious toleration which is now extended to all religious bodies in Mauritius. Since that period he has been labouring earnestly and successfully in the evangelisation of the negro and coloured population. He opened a school in connexion with his mission, and some of the wealthiest men of colour in the colony owe their position to the instruction thus imparted. The emancipation of the slaves added largely to the number of his adherents, and there are now four congregations connected with the religious body which he represents. These congregations have places of worship at Port Louis, at Moka, at Plaines Wilhelmes, and at Grande Rivière. Mr Le Brun has devoted all his time and talents to the elevation and Christianisation of the coloured people, who owe him a debt of gratitude which they can never sufficiently repay. He is now assisted in his labours by his two sons, and almost all the Protestants among the coloured population are members of his church.

In 1851, a minister of the Church of Scotland was appointed to Mauritius. For many years before, a sum had been set aside in the annual estimates of expenditure as the salary of a Presbyterian minister, but the Scotchmen in the colony failed to profit by this concession. At length, a few of them, previously connected with the Church of England, but dissatisfied with that Church as it then existed in the colony, petitioned the Colonial Committee of the Church of Scotland for a minister. It does not appear that any Presbyterian minister had ever visited the colony before this, except the Rev. Mr Nesbit, a highly-respected missionary of the Free Church. He touched there on his way to India, and officiated in English in Mr Le Brun's chapel. He appears to have made a profound impression upon his audience, several of whom still speak of his earnest and impressive eloquence. The Scotch congregation met in the Court-house, which had been kindly conceded by the judges, till the beginning of 1856, when they took possession of St Andrew's Church, a handsome building in the early Norman style. There is not a large number of Presbyterians in the colony, but there are good and useful men amongst them, who take an active interest in the spiritual welfare of the poorer classes. About twenty natives of India were instructed in the elementary truths of Christianity, and baptized by the founder of the Scotch Church, who left the colony at the close of 1856.

There are three Associations, that have been recently formed, in connexion with the Protestant Churches of Mauritius, which deserve some notice. The Mauritius Church Association was formed by Dr Chapman, on the occasion of his visit to the colony in 1850. The object of this association has been already mentioned. It is supported exclusively by members of the Church of England, and has contributed largely to the erection of churches at Mahèbourg and Pamplemousses. Under the able presidency of the present Bishop, it will, no doubt, prove still more highly useful, and fully serve the purpose for which it was instituted.

The Mauritius Auxiliary Branch of the British and Foreign Bible Society was formed on the 25th of May

1852, under the following circumstances. On the arrival of the minister of the Church of Scotland in 1851, he found that the supply of Scriptures which he had brought with him was insufficient to meet the wants of his own congregation, and that there was no place in the colony where copies could be bought. Anxious to remedy this state of things, he secured the co-operation and assistance of several influential Protestants, and a public meeting, the largest ever assembled in the colony, was held in the Freemasons' Hall. Interesting addresses were delivered by ministers and members of the different Protestant Churches, an Auxiliary Branch of the Bible Society was formed, and office-bearers appointed. Copies of the Holy Scriptures, in French, English, Chinese, and in all the different languages spoken by the Indian immigrants, were procured, and natives of Madagascar and India employed as colporteurs. About 10,000 Scriptures, or portions of Scripture, have been sold or distributed among the inhabitants, and the good effects produced by the reading of the Word of God have been evidenced by the formation of one Creole and two Indian congregations, that owe their existence to the labours of the Bible Society and its agents. It would be difficult to over-estimate the amount of good that has been effected by this truly catholic Society, and it ought to be the earnest prayer of all who are interested in the progress of divine truth, that the Word of God, which is quick and powerful, and sharper than any two-edged sword, may find its way into every hamlet and cottage in this colony, and make

Mauritius resemble a garden of the Lord, which, watered by the Spirit, shall produce abundantly the peaceable fruits of righteousness.

The Seamen's Friend Society was formed in 1854, for the purpose of ministering to the spiritual wants of the 12,000 seamen who visit the harbour of Port Louis every year. The arrival of Dr Ryan, and the appointment of Mr Bichard as seamen's chaplain, supersede in a great measure, the necessity for the Society's operations, and the efforts of its members were directed mainly to raising the funds required for opening a Sailors' Home. The dens of infamy and crime, in which seamen who left their ships in Mauritius were obliged to lodge, cannot be described, and the arrival of Commodore Trotter, the officer commanding at the Cape station in November 1856, was deemed a favourable opportunity for calling upon all Christians to unite in trying to provide a remedy for this great and crying evil. An influential meeting was held, and a large sum of money readily subscribed. The Government agreed to pay from the Colonial Treasury a sum equal to that raised by private subscription, and in this way the funds necessary for opening a Sailors' Home were soon raised. The services of a highly-respectable man, well acquainted with the character and habits of seamen, were secured as superintendent, and the sailors have had the good sense to frequent the Home in preference to their former haunts, some of which have been closed.

CHAPTER VIII.

Madagascar, Description of—Mission of 1816—Progress of Christianity
—Death of King Radama in 1828—National Assembly of 1835—
Persecution of the Native Christians—Their Fortitude and Faith—
Attack on the Fort of Tamatave—The Queen's Answer to the Go-
vernor of Mauritius—Conversion of Prince Rakoto—Persecution of
1849—Proclamation against Christianity—Martyrs in Madagascar
—Report of the Queen's Resignation—Visit of the Rev. W. Ellis
and Mr Cameron—Removal of Traffic between Madagascar and
Mauritius—The Queen's Letter—Church of Rome in Madagascar—
Report of a French Armament for the Invasion of the Island—Fresh
Persecution of the Christians—Conclusion.

In the course of this work, we have had frequent occasion to allude to the neighbouring island of Madagascar,
between which and Mauritius the most intimate relations have existed, and a brief notice of the persecutions
of the native Christians by the present queen may not
be out of place. Many of these men have found refuge
in Mauritius, and two of them were highly useful as
colporteurs among the Creole population. The following statement is derived chiefly from a small work
published at the Cape by Mr Cameron, who spent many
years as a lay missionary in Madagascar, before the ex-
pulsion of the Christian teachers, and who again visited
the island in 1853.

Madagascar is a large island, about 900 miles long
by 300 broad, situated opposite the mouth of the Zam-

besi, the river recently explored by the indefatigable Livingstone, and separated from the mainland by the Mozambique Channel. It is inhabited by two distinct races, the one of Arab, the other of Negro origin. The capital, Antananarivo, is situated in a district called Ankova, near the centre of the island. In this city, a mission connected with the London Missionary Society was established in 1818, with the consent and approval of Radama, the king. A grammar and dictionary of the native language were compiled; schools were opened in the different villages; native youths instructed in Christianity by the missionaries, who preached the gospel from place to place; and in 1826 a printing-press was erected. Thousands learned to read, and the seed seemed to have fallen in a propitious soil. But persecution has ever followed in the wake of Christianity. The old saying, that "the blood of the martyrs is the seed of the Church," was to hold true here as elsewhere. Radama died in 1828, a heathen, favourable to Christianity only because he considered Christianity favourable to the development of the resources of the country and of the intellect of his subjects. The queen, his successor, for two years tolerated Christianity, which made rapid progress, especially among the lower classes. The jealousy of the old heathen Conservative party was excited, and their influence employed with the queen to suppress Christianity. On the 1st of March 1835, a sort of National Assembly was held, at which it was resolved that Christianity should be extirpated, and the profession of it treated as a capital crime. The seeds of Christianity had taken too deep root, however, to be eradicated so easily. Many knew in whom they had trusted, and felt that they ought to' obey God rather than man. Several were condemned to imprisonment and slavery, immediately after the National Assembly of 1835, though none actually suffered death till 1837. The first martyr was one of that sex who were the last at the cross, the first at the sepulchre. She walked to the place of execution singing hymns, and met her fate with Christian fortitude. One only of her fellow-Christians accompanied her to her place of martyrdom. Her example decided him in the profession of the Christian faith, and he suffered soon after. This man's wife was then seized and tortured, along with another person, till they disclosed the names of the principal Christians. Most of these concealed themselves in places inaccessible to the queen's forces, and six of them, aided by their friends, reached Tamatave, the principal sea-port, and escaped to Mauritius. Those who remained were exposed to great hardships, and an attempt was made in 1842, by a missionary of the name of Griffiths, who had returned to the island, to effect their escape. Every arrangement was made. Two natives well acquainted with the country were to conduct them to Tamatave, from which they could escape to Mauritius. When one-half of the journey was completed, their conductors betrayed them into the hands of the queen's troops, and nine of them were put to death in the most barbarous and revolting manner. Mr Griffiths, the missionary, was compelled to leave the island immediately.

After this period, there seems to have been a cessation for some time in the persecution of the native Christians. The fate of their companions had rendered them more cautious. At the same time their thirst for the Word of God continued as ardent as before. New Testaments were supplied at times through vessels trading between Tamatave and Mauritius. This trade, however, was interrupted by an unfortunate and unsuccessful attack made by one English and two French ships of war upon the native fort at Tamatave. In the beginning of 1845, the queen had published a proclamation, to the effect that all foreigners remaining in the island after a certain specified time, would become subject to the laws of the country. In making this proclamation, she only exercised a right which belongs to every independent sovereign. The commanders of the vessels alluded to tried in vain to obtain some relaxation of this law in favour of their countrymen resident in the island. They then opened a severe fire on the fort, and after cannonading it for several hours, they landed and endeavoured to take possession of it. They were repulsed with considerable loss, and the bodies of the slain were decapitated, and their heads insultingly stuck upon poles. There was a touch of savage grandeur in the queen's reply to a remonstrance from the Governor of Mauritius :—" Each of all the kings of the earth has had his land apportioned to him by God, and each rules his own land in his own way. Our queen attempts not to rule your queen, and your queen must not attempt to rule ours." After this

unfortunate affair, all exportation of produce from the
island was strictly prohibited, and little was known of
the condition of the native Christians, save through
letters occasionally received by their friends in Mauritius, or through fugitives to the same place. The ways
of God in promoting His truth are very wonderful. In
the apostolic age, Christianity found its way into the
palaces of Rome through the medium of slaves, who
instructed their heathen masters. Something like this
occurred also at Madagascar. God wanted a protector
for these poor Christians, and He chose the son of their
persecutor. Rakoto, the queen's only son, was instructed in Christianity by one of the Christians who
held office in the palace, and made an open profession
of his faith. He was induced to do this by the following singular circumstance. He had been told that
neither the idol Ramahavaly nor the temple which contained it could be consumed with fire, and repeated this
remark within the hearing of his Christian instructor.
Both were speedily reduced to ashes. The prince witnessed the fire from the balcony of his house, and from
that time renounced idolatry. The prince soon after
succeeded in gaining over to the truth a son of the
queen's sister, named Ramouja, a man of great influence at the court, and both have ever since continued
to protect the Christians. A brother of Ramouja's,
named Rambosalama, the adopted son of the queen,
before the birth of Rakoto, remained violently opposed
to Christianity. He seems to have taken an active part
in instigating the queen to begin that severe persecution

which was undertaken against Christianity in 1849. The houses used as places of worship were destroyed, and several of the principal Christians apprehended. Those who confessed, and promised to renounce the truth, were either pardoned or condemned to pay certain fines, while those who adhered to the truth, were put to death, chiefly by being hurled from a precipice. Christianity was prohibited in the following terms :— " There are things which shall not be done, saith the queen. The saying to others, Believe and obey the Gospel ; the practice of baptism ; the keeping of the Sabbath as a day of rest ; the refusing to swear by one's father, or mother, or sister, or brother, and the refusing to be sworn, with a stubbornness like that of bullocks, or stones, or wood ; the taking of a little bread and of the juice of the grape, and the asking a blessing to rest on the crown of your head ; and kneeling down upon the ground and praying, and rising from prayer with drops of water falling from your noses, and with tears rolling down your eyes." What an affecting picture of the administration of the Lord's Supper in that remote island ! It will remind the reader of Pliny the younger's description of the manners and customs of the Christians in his province, or of the Scottish Covenanters kneeling on the mountain heather, and partaking of the sacred elements beside some solitary lake, far from the pursuit of their persecutors.

Nearly two thousand persons confessed themselves to be Christians. All of these were punished in their persons or properties, and fourteen were put to death in the following manner :—They were carried to the top of a rock, where criminals guilty of capital crimes were wont to be conducted, before being precipitated to the bottom. Persons guilty of the vilest offences were associated with them, so as to degrade them in the eyes of their countrymen, and cast ridicule upon their religion. Each in succession was suspended by a rope over the fearful precipice, and life offered to him if he would recant ; but they all deemed it better to depart and to be with Christ. Some of these devoted men seem, like Stephen, to have been favoured with such glimpses of the Redeemer's glory as filled their souls with transports of holy joy, and led them to welcome death as the greatest boon. Their dying words made a deep and lasting impression upon their countrymen. Only one young woman, who had been a favourite of the queen's, was spared. She was placed in a prominent position from which she could witness the deaths of her companions in succession, and it is reported by some that her resolution failed her so that she renounced Christianity, by others, that the queen extended to her a free pardon, without any such recantation. In the course of the same year 1849, eighteen other persons were put to death on account of their adherence to Christianity, their property confiscated, and their families reduced to a state of slavery. But they " counted all things but loss for the knowledge of Christ and Him crucified." With a spirit similar to that which animated the early martyrs, they were prepared to endure all, and to give up all, rather than renounce that Saviour whose precious blood had cleansed them from all sin. And thus "they overcame by the blood of the Lamb."

A large quantity of New Testaments and portions of Scripture in Malagashe, published by the British and Foreign Bible Society, had been entrusted to the care of the Rev. J. Le Brun at Port Louis, in the expectation that some opening might present itself for the introduction of them into Madagascar. From 1845 to 1853, only a few opportunities occurred of introducing small quantities of Scriptures into Madagascar. The few Frenchmen who had been allowed to remain in the island were opposed to the introduction of the Bible and the return of the missionaries, because these were opposed to their licentious and sinful lives. In Mauritius also, any attempt at Christianising Madagascar would meet with little favour, because the queen's prohibition of all foreign trade was erroneously imputed to her jealousy or dislike of the missionaries. A fugitive from Madagascar was employed in 1852 to convey Scriptures to his countrymen who still adhered to Christianity, but information of his design was given to the authorities, and such a strict surveillance observed, that he was obliged to return without having effected his purpose. The same year, rumours reached England from Mauritius, to the effect that the queen, who has been for many years the slave of intemperate habits, had resigned the crown in favour of her son Rakoto, who had proclaimed toleration to Christianity throughout his dominions. In consequence of these rumours, the Rev. W. Ellis and Mr Cameron, residing at Cape Town, both formerly connected with the Mission to Madagascar, were sent to Mauritius, to examine into their truth. The result was not satisfactory, but they resolved to visit Madagascar, and arrived at Tamatave in the month of July. They discovered through a native convert, who introduced himself to their notice, that the persecution of 1849 had failed to extirpate Christianity, there being still about 800 persons in the neighbourhood of 'the capital who adhered to it, and a church, containing about sixty members, regularly organised. Few copies of the Scriptures had escaped the search made for them in 1849, but these had been preserved with a carefulness that shewed how highly they were appreciated. A New Testament was exhibited by Mr Ellis, after his return to Mauritius. It was so much soiled, and worn, and patched, that it was difficult to recognise the original work, and the sight of it might have touched the hearts of many careless professors of religion, who neglect their Bibles, with a feeling of shame. It is now, we believe, at the depôt of the British and Foreign Bible Society in London. In June 1853, a memorial, signed by the members of the Chamber of Commerce at Port Louis and others, was transmitted to the Queen of Madagascar, petitioning that the ports of that island might be re-opened for foreign trade, and the friendly relations formerly existing between the two places renewed. This memorial was conveyed to Madagascar in July, and immediately received the following gracious reply from the queen :—

"ANTANANARIVO, *July* 1853.

"To P. A. Wiehè, Esq., President of the Chamber of Commerce, and to Davy and Robinson, and Jamet, and all their associates.

"I am to inform you that I am in possession of the letter written by you in June 1853 to the Queen of Madagascar. Also that I have made known to the Queen of Madagascar the words (or contents) of your letter.

"And this is the reason why commerce is closed, and that you have to ask that traffic may be re-opened: Romain Desfosses and Wm. Kelly, and their companions, in three ships, on a former occasion fired guns upon us, intending to take our country, and this made us extremely angry.

"Now, when they make a payment of 15,000 dollars for injury done, commerce will be re-opened. For those who attacked us are not people unknown, but people that came from the English and French. And further, any others may pay that sum, if the payment be made as coming from (or for) them,—and even in that case commerce will be re-opened.

"And I beg to tell you plainly, that, whether commerce be re-opened or remain closed, we have no enemies beyond the sea, for all that are there are our relatives and friends.—Farewell, &c., says

RAMIKIETAKA,
13th Honor, and Officer of the Palace."

On receiving this answer, which in clearness and brevity might serve as a model to be imitated by European diplomatists, the Chamber of Commerce soon collected the amount demanded, and Mr Cameron and another person were employed to convey it to the queen. They were successful in their mission, and returned to Mauritius in November with a cargo of bullocks. The trade between the two colonies has continued ever since, but no opening has yet been presented for the introduction of the Word of God on a large scale, or the resumption of missionary labour. The French have an establishment on Nossé Bay, and priests connected with the Roman Catholic Mission to the eastern coast of Africa, have endeavoured to obtain a footing in the island, and to win over the native Christians to Romanism, by representing their system as identical with that in which they had been instructed by the missionaries. They signally failed, however, in this attempt. " To the law and to the testimony," was the motto of these primitive men, and as the tenets of Romanism were found irreconcileable with the teachings of the Bible, they were at once rejected. The French have always been anxious, since their colonisation of Mauritius and Bourbon, to establish themselves permanently in Madagascar. Soon after the conclusion of the Crimean war, it was reported that the Emperor of France was about to fit out a large armament for the subjugation of this island. The report probably was connected with the return to France of a French merchant established at Mauritius, and largely connected with the Madagascar trade, who visited the island, and had an interview with the young prince Rakoto. This prince lives in daily apprehension of a violent death at the hands of the queen's adopted son, to whom allusion has already been made, as a violent opponent of Christianity. It is related by Mr Cameron, that about six months before his visit to the island, Rakoto purchased a quantity of red cloth, such as is often used to wrap the bodies of the royal dead. "The queen asked him what he meant by purchasing such cloth? He said to her that he considered his life in danger from a quarter which she well knew, and that if he must die in such a way, he would prefer dying while she was yet alive. She only said, 'My Rakoto, what makes you say so?'" This extract from Mr Cameron's narrative, published at Cape Town in 1854, will shew that the prince was then apprehensive of a violent death. The Frenchman to whom we allude, seems to have worked upon his fears till he induced him to write a letter to the Emperor of France, requesting him to take the island of Madagascar under his protection, and to establish Christianity. This letter was delivered to the Emperor, and soon after the report originated that an army was to be fitted out for the invasion of Madagascar. As yet no attempt had been made, and if made, it is doubtful whether it would be successful. The Malagashes are a brave and warlike race, possessed of great physical strength and powers of endurance. The interior of the island abounds in mountains and inaccessible forests, which cavalry and artillery could never pierce. A recent fact shews that the authorities are extremely jealous of any attempt, on the part of any foreign power, to obtain a permanent footing in the colony. A French firm in Mauritius obtained permission to work a coal mine in Madagascar. For self-protection, they built a small fort, and had the temerity to display the French flag upon it. The authorities commanded them to remove it, and on their refusal, a party of native soldiers destroyed the fort, and several of its defenders were slain. The Malagashe authorities had undoubtedly justice on their side. The French had no more right to build a fort and to display their flag in Madagascar, than they would have to do so in Mauritius. The attempt in either case would be suppressed, and the guilty parties punished, without exciting any sympathy.

The Rev. W. Ellis re-visited Madagascar towards the close of 1856, but it does not yet appear that his visit produced any good effect, or has been followed with any important result. It is a pleasant sight to see this devoted missionary, who is now well advanced in years, ready to renounce all the comforts of civilised life, to undertake a voyage of many thousand miles, and to expose himself to death in a heathen land, not from the desire of fame or of personal aggrandisement, but in obedience to the command of his Master, "Go ye and preach the gospel unto all nations." Accounts have recently reached this country that a fresh persecution of the native Christians has broken out in Madagascar, and that about fifty of them have been put to death. All who are interested in the evangelisation of the heathen, and the establishment of Christ's kingdom on earth, should be earnest in their prayers, that this island, now the habitation of cruelty, may soon be brought within the pale of His Church, and that religious toleration and deliverance from persecution may be extended to those who have retained their adhesion to Christianity, amid trials and sufferings unequalled in the annals of the Church since the persecutions of the early Christians by the Roman Emperors.

THE END.